Townframe

Community Development Series

Series Editor: Richard P. Dober, AIP

CDS/38

Townframe

ENVIRONMENTS FOR ADAPTIVE HOUSING

Guntis Plēsums

University of Oregon

Dowden, Hutchinson & Ross, Inc.

Stroudsburg, Pennsylvania

To Jāna and Kārla

This work was made possible by a grant from the Graham
Foundation for Advanced Studies in the Fine Arts.

78 79 80 5 4 3 2 1
Manufactured in the United States of America.

Library of Congress Cataloging in Publication Data

Plēsums, Guntis.
  Townframe.
  (Community development series ; v. 38)
  Includes index.
  1. Architecture—Environmental aspects. 2. Architecture—Human fac-
tors. I. Title.
NA2542.35.P55   720   77-20679
ISBN 0-87933-303-0

Series Editor's Foreword

Townframe by Guntis Plēsums defines and explores technologies that can be used to develop large and complex physical environments. It is an adventuresome work that should extend our ideas about how machine made parts could be assembled into human scale habitats.

The theme is one that has fascinated designers since earliest times. The Hanging Gardens of Babylon, empire cities along the Nile, archaic and classical Chinese precincts, Vitruvian renaissance towns come readily to mind as places where such *structuring* is used as an organizing principle in large area architecture. In these examples we can see modular brick, wood, stone fitting together into workable space patterns. Materials and methods are ancient to be sure, but not unsophisticated when measured by the then available science technology, and management.

In recent decades there has been no less interest in the subject, but, in the main, little accomplishment. The work of Buckminster Fuller, Paolo Soleri, Peter Cook and the Archigram movement, and Japanese megastructures all give evidence of what might be done. The diversity of thought, keenly honed by creative minds, unfortunately lies unapplied, sometimes dismissed as guruism, counterculture or pop art, often economically impractical, or frightening to those who see the resulting environment as a Kafkaesque future, or worse as a Popular Science magazine cover come into full fruition.

Plēsums' efforts cannot be easily disentangled from such misinterpretations and restraints. A saving grace is his willingness to confront these questions directly, for example, the issue of control versus choice in constructing enormous, connected, multipurpose architecture.

Valuable in its own right, *Townframe* is doubly welcomed because the question of control and choice in design processes is central to many books published in the Community Development Series, viz active user and client involvement in shaping the environment.

Plēsums also touches on several other CDS concerns: the systematic searching out of relationships between design and human behavior; ecological ethics, particularly the interrelatedness of design decisions at all scales in the built environment; and an interest in not just finding appropriate solutions to design problems, but also in establishing ways and means for having those solutions implemented.

For all these purposes, books continue to be a useful way for professionals and their clients to share information, expert advice, and experience. Written by and for practioners, CDS books are thus offered to planners, architects, landscape architects, engineers, designers and others who can benefit by having such knowledge in a readily convenient format.

Richard P. Dober, AIP

Acknowledgments

It is not possible to recognize all the people who in one way or another contributed to the conception and realization of this work. I would, however, acknowledge my indebtedness to:

Carter H. Manny, Jr., Director of Graham Foundation for Advanced Studies in the Fine Arts, for his patience with this study. The grant allowed me to undertake the research project and to do major portions of the book. Māra Plēsums, my wife, who not only edited and typed the text but did not refrain from registering her reservations and questioning some presumptions. Her patience during these years provided the necessary milieu for this work. The Office of Scientific and Scholarly Research, University of Oregon, for awarding funds to defray some of the model-building and photographing expenses.

Brian Nelson, Michael Johnson, and Rober Segal, students, University of Oregon, for assisting with the construction of the large model. The students of my Architectural Design Studios at the University of Oregon who, for several terms, tested some aspects of the model framework through their design proposals or who explored similar possibilities and parallel issues.

Ronald Lovinger, Professor of Landscape Architecture, University of Oregon, for his enthusiasm and support during our joint studio experiment. Richard P. Dober, editor of Community Development Series, who persuaded me to write the book and who gave it direction. Charles S. Hutchinson, Jr., publisher, who assisted with the production and contractual matters in a reassuring way throughout the preparation of this work. Juris Mazutis, engineer-poet, for giving the manuscript a most thorough reading. The students of Kansas State University for enduring a visitor and contributing their design probes.

Contents

Townframe

1

An Argument

INTRODUCTION

No single factor is likely to stop suburban sprawl, and the problems associated with this sprawl are well enough known that we need not dwell on them here. The amenities of a house in a natural setting are tempered by the socially deprived suburban environment, distance to the city center, and disastrous impact on available land, to name but a few consequences of the "American dream." Social problems have likewise migrated from the inner city to suburbia.

Some forty years ago Le Corbusier proposed the construction of artificial sites (Figure 1–1), and there have been a number of other experiments since then. Few high-density housing prototypes can favorably compete with the amenities of a house in its natural setting. Generally available new apartments and their surroundings are simply not a match for the detached house. Despite the fact that here in the United States we are almost able to produce a sufficient number of housing units, housing constitutes the foremost unsolved problem in architecture. A viable high-density residential model remains an elusive goal.

The urge to choose, to structure, to manipulate one's own immediate environment is one of man's most compelling drives. Our instinctively felt right to shape our lives is under continuous threat. Intentionally and unintentionally we are subjected to regimentation in every aspect of our lives. This regimentation is nowhere more evident than in the built environment, particularly in mass housing. Although the tendency toward standard, uniform housing is by no means a recent occurrence, the advent of more efficient production, construction, scheduling, and marketing makes prospects for a human environment bleak, to say the least. Current trends in industrialization point toward a simplistic interpretation of this process and will further contribute to a monstrous monotony and thereby rule out opportunities for control of one's private realm.

Figure 1–1
Le Corbusier's 1931–1934 proposal for Algiers. Note: According to the designer, "Here are 'artificial sites', vertical garden cities . . . . The architectural aspect is stunning! The most absolute diversity, within unity. Every architect will build his villa as he likes; what does it matter to the whole if a Moorish-style villa flanks another in Louis XVIth or in Italian Renaissance?" (See Le Corbusier, *La Ville Radieuse* first published in 1933, reprinted in 1964, © Vincent, Freal & Cie, Paris. All rights reserved.)

The increasing scale of housing projects, the short time available for design and construction, and the anonymity and turnover of the occupants no longer assure a fit between the needs of the user and his physical environment. Apartments and houses are built to house generalized categories of people. Furthermore, requirements only become apparent

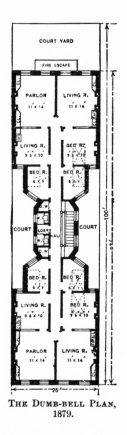

COURT YARD

FIRE ESCAPE

PARLOR 11' x 14' LIVING R. 11' x 14'

LIVING R. 9' 6" x 10' BED R.

BED R. 6' x 5' BED R. 6' x 5'

COURT LOBBY HALL COURT

BED R. BED R.

LIVING R. 9' 6" x 10' BED R. 9' 6" x 10'

PARLOR 11' x 14' LIVING R. 11' x 14'

THE DUMB-BELL PLAN, 1879.

Figure 1-2
Plan of model tenements widely copied from 1879 to about 1900, despite an almost unanimous condemnation of tenements. Note: The Dumb-bell plan was considered one of the worst types ever constructed. (See Robert W. De Forest and Lawrence Veiller, eds., *The Tenement House Problem* (New York: Macmillan, 1903), vol. 1, p. 101.)

through occupation. There are too many contradictory and changing needs, too many physical and cultural contexts, and too many constantly evolving values for any one applicable residential architecture and building system. Any attempt to program for individual needs—that is, any attempt to come up with the criteria for the ideal dwelling—will undoubtedly end in omissions, extravagances, contradictions, and even oppressive conditions for some people.

Existing residential prototypes do not recognize the pluralistic nature of contemporary society. We tend to satisfy common physical needs and consequently mold people to fit the prescribed norms. The ideal situation would call for as many more or less different dwellings as there are people. Of course some of the differences are small, but in the course of living they become significant. Moving to a different apartment becomes unavoidable for some people and results in uprooting, frustrations, and expense. Surely, for any outside design and construction service to cope with the initial needs and the subsequent alterations of everyone is impossible.

Consequently, we have two extremes: The ultimate plan and individualized service are unrealistic and unattainable. There is no ideal "final solution" in housing, and producing custom-made dwellings that would remain appropriate for any length of time is an impossible task.

Obsolete Construction

Much of the existing built environment is inadequate and obsolete, and some of our new construction is contributing to this obsolescence. The substandard quality of our older buildings is well recognized. Notwithstanding their often desirable characteristics, such as human scale, variety, opportunities for personalizing, and so forth, these dwellings are permanently

"locked in" without any possibility of additions, room rearrangements, or some other change.

If we look at turn-of-the-century tenements, for example, we see that the load-bearing masonry walls more than any other property make renovating these often structurally sound buildings impossible. The small, dark interior rooms facing into air shafts are not acceptable today by any standards; yet such buildings were occupied by middle-class tenants at one time. Some, like the unfortunate Dumb-bell plan (Figure 1-2), which was widely used after winning a competition in 1879, resulted in the most horrid living conditions. The legacy of these structures is still with us. Inadequate mechanical and electrical systems, inherent fire hazards, and a general condition of disrepair further contribute to their obsolescence. Of course, regardless of their condition, these buildings and neighborhoods quickly acquire certain cultural and psychological connotations from which the inhabitants would rather escape anyway.

Less often recognized is the built-in obsolescence of current construction. Dwellings and their surroundings are built and landscaped without adequate and acceptable planning and design standards. Despite our ever-increasing volume of construction, most recently built environments are inconsequential in their contribution to a more human environment and, in fact, detrimental to the well-being of man. Their disappearance would not be a shattering loss to civilization.

Buildings are put together with shoddy craftsmanship. The bulk of current construction is a blatant waste of valuable resources and constitutes pollution of the worst kind. This domain is controlled and corrupted by profiteers who use mortgage policies and the tax structure to their advantage. Many current practices are the consequence of a consumptive lifestyle that demands immediate gratification. Buildings are built to last the duration of the mortgage, which keeps getting shorter and shorter, and they virtually disintegrate thereafter. Buildings are exploited and then written off as tax losses. Partial or complete destruction of buildings often represents the only "change" we can visualize. Recycling, if it exists at all, consists of reprocessing or crude salvaging of a few materials and items. The disposable environment is a sad reality.

Buildings as Systems

Buildings are built without recognition of the varying life cycles of their systems,[1] although there have always been buildings that have more or less contained long-term and short-term systems. A life cycle is the usable time period of a building's part or system, such as a chimney, the roofing, a lock, or the plumbing. The awareness of such life cycles has not played a conscientious and significant role in building design.

Although space can be defined using light or some other imaginary means, buildings and other structures consist of physical systems. These systems, their countless subsystems, and the resulting hierarchies constitute an ecology of construction. This interrelationship between these various systems and their relative importance and life cycles is what concerns us. It is of supreme importance in establishing the life span of the building and its various systems.

If we examine any ordinary building, we are well aware of the relative importance of structure. Without structure, architectural space can not be formed. Yet we persistently continue to use restrictive systems, such as load-bearing masonry or wood stud walls. Distinctions between protective enclosures, partitions, and structure are obscured in return for initial cost savings.

Such practices characterize the design and construction of all other major systems, but do not extend to the smaller items. Interchangeability of doors, hardware, and fixtures is commonly accepted.

We do not think of producing light bulbs integral with the wiring; yet we persist in embedding electrical wiring in the construction. The mechanical and electrical systems have a particularly short life cycle. They also require frequent maintenance. Witness the fact that wiring in post-World War II houses is inadequate because the increase in household appliances was not anticipated. Yet we go on building as if every part of the house is to last equally long.

No complex adaptive system will succeed in adapting in a reasonable amount of time unless the adaptation can proceed subsystem by subsystem, each subsystem relatively independent of the others.[2]

The prevailing construction practice in its disregard of the role of each and every system and subsystem not only affects the life span of the building, but is of paramount importance in the evolution of user-controlled habitats. Without recognition of this ecological order in construction, manipulation of one's dwelling will remain an expensive, wasteful, and frustrating endeavor, and industrialization will proceed on its present course of producing containers for humans.

Industrialization

There is a widely shared belief among those advocating industrialization in building that once industrialization is a reality, all our housing problems and perhaps even some of the social problems will disappear. Industrialization, according to its most passionate advocates, will supply people with their dream homes and keep these dwellings contemporary with continuous editions of new models. This is consumerism pushed to its limits.

Although standardization and industrialization in building in one form or another has existed throughout history and has produced some fascinating buildings and structures, its very recent trend is most

alarming. Standardization is not recognized as a vehicle for infinite combinations, but as a more efficient method for turning out a larger number of identical units—for example, mobile homes that are fixed in size and shape, uniformly finished, and unadaptable. This approach, rather than a systems-oriented attitude towards building, has already endowed us with repetitive high-rise towers, Levittowns, and mobile-home communities. Now we are likely to end up with suburban, medium- and high-density "modular" homes (Figure 1–3).

There is absolutely no doubt that industrialization in building is necessary and inevitable. Industrialization and consequently automation promise to free man from the drudgery of repetitive tasks; it can turn out a large number of products, control quality, and guarantee standardization, to name but a few of its attributes. Industrialization in building, however, should be the means towards an end and not the end itself. This simple truth is being ignored by the advocates of "modular" and mobile homes. This industry is not solving dire long-range housing problems but contributing to them.

THE JAPANESE EXAMPLE

A model suitable for user manipulation exists. The Japanese house has not been equalled by any contemporary building system. The tradition it represents remains an unparalleled source of inspiration and a measure of quality. It offers proof that industrialization can follow a more human course.

The purpose in presenting this discussion here is not to advocate copying Japanese houses and forms. The Japanese house evolved hundreds of years ago in a different culture. It no longer supports present Japanese lifestyles and never fully protected inhabitants from the elements. The forms, the spaces, and the building system could not possibly suit our present

Figure 1-3
"Skye Rise Terrace" in St. Paul, Minnesota. Note: According to the developer's flyer, this project was the "...nation's first multistory mobile-home development ..."; unfortunately, the inevitable extension of this grotesque product soon mushroomed in other metropolitan areas as well. (Photograph by Valdemārs Plēsums.)

or foreseeable needs. Nevertheless, it provides us with some invaluable lessons.

The virtues of the Japanese house are too numerous to list here.[3] What concerns us, however, is the scale of the building system and the ease with which it could be manipulated by the inhabitants. No architect was needed, and the owner did not choose among ready-made houses. All design decisions as to room sizes, relationships, landscaping, openings, built-ins, and so forth were made by the owner with the help of the carpenter. Of course, these decisions were made within prescribed rules and accepted standards (Figures 1-4 and 1-5).

Japanese, and to a lesser degree Chinese, tradi-

Figure 1-5
Prefabricated roof members for a Japanese house. Note: Precisely carved joints and markings facilitate quick assembly. Carefully protected with straw mats during shipping the components can be easily handled by a single person without the need for heavy equipment.

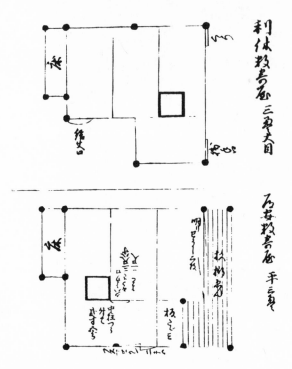

Figure 1-4
Possible teahouse layouts. (From a woodblock-printed nineteenth-century Japanese carpenter's manual.)

tional building has recognized a hierarchy in building systems. The construction system is the very media that creates architectural form and space. This construction is the source of aesthetic sensation and intellectual satisfaction. The most sophisticated villas, such as the Katsura Imperial Palace, and the most humble dwelling used the same system (Figures 1-6 and 1-7). Every element has a distinct place in this order. Subsystems stem from acceptance of more permanent major systems. Elements in this hierarchy are replaced when worn out or changed with the turn of seasons or in response to some other event. The house and its inhabitants share in the rhythm of life.

Parts of remaining structures with all the intricate joinery were used to construct new and often quite different buildings. The carefully detailed wood com-

Figure 1-6
The Katsura Imperial Palace in Kyoto, Japan. Note: The same materials and essentially the same systems were used in this construction as in other buildings of the times. Started in 1620 by Prince Toshihito and completed by 1658, the buildings and garden were greatly influenced by descriptions in Lady Murasaki's *The Tale of Genji* (c. 1026–1031). As a vision of an ideal place, the palace is exquisitely refined and ranks as one of the great monuments of architecture.

Figure 1-7
The Semura house in Kanazawa, Japan. Note: This home is just an ordinary dwelling of the nineteenth century. Although different from any other house in its spatial configuration, openings and relationship to the outside, it nevertheless shares the same building system with millions of other houses. Only time and refinement separate this humble house from its distant predecessor, the Katsura Imperial Palace. (Photograph by Richard Smith, University of Oregon.)

ponents were valuable. New temple compounds were started by moving the remaining structures from temples destroyed in a calamity. Buildings or building components were given as gifts by rulers to secure political favors. Japanese history is full of such descriptions. Poverty dictated recycling of the more lasting building systems and repair of the fragile elements.

The homogenous Japanese culture, in fact, discouraged change; yet the building system embodied potential for it within the limitations of known and accepted methods. The primary systems have withstood the ravages of time, and the subsystems have undergone considerable transformation. This adaptability and the self-regulating quality of Japanese architecture deserve the most careful study.

CHANGEABLE BUILDINGS

Our energy crisis and impending shortage of resources will compel us to follow the Japanese example. Existing alternatives seem to be quite clear: Either little will get built or our dwellings will get even more tacky. Would not the use of adaptability and individual choice and control as the guiding principles in design of housing thus be advisable? Recognition that some physical systems are relatively constant while others are variable in domestic architecture, and for that matter in construction generally, is inevitable.

We need to look at changes in buildings as positive phenomena. This attitude is difficult if every part of a building is conceived as permanent, perfect, and untouchable, and if the building itself is held to be a finite object or a work of art where personalization is viewed by the designer as an unfortunate and destructive event, which it often is, simply because he has not anticipated and provided for it. The aesthetics of changes in buildings have yet to be explored.

Change for the sake of change is just as absurd. It destroys the security that comes with known surroundings, identity with times past, the assurance of continuity, and perhaps the very meaning of life. Absence of clues about past events casts doubts on the reality of the present and the possibility of a future. Yet the very presence of history may be an oppressive reminder of a more primitive past to those who have to confront it day in and day out. The line between permanence and change is delicate indeed, but the relatively permanent must be integrated with the changeable.

As is often argued, well-designed places are supportive of a range of activities, and such houses can be possessed by a multitude of inhabitants. There is no doubt that such places will remain as elevating experiences, but then how many such houses and particularly apartments are being built? The bulk of built environment, especially mass housing, is unfit to live in. Experience also shows that these supportive houses are extensive. That one should be able to find the proper place for one's activity in a thoughtfully designed house is the argument most often given. Whether we will be able to afford to purchase and maintain such extensive dwellings is doubtful, but surely there must be a way of achieving more with less.

The issue is complex. Man's need to change his immediate environment is one manifestation of possession (Figure 1–8), as is well stated by Habraken:

... alterations were not always done for functional purposes. They were done to keep up with the times or because notions about living changed, because one could not identify with what one took over or because it belonged to a different generation. The occupant would rarely have been interested in aesthetic values, and anyway such considerations would change as much as the houses. But the house was an important means of illustrating his position in life. It was his social expression, his way of establishing his ego. For this it was necessary that the occupant should possess his dwelling in the fullest sense of the word. If changes were made it was not in

order to preserve the building, but because one could not afford to pull down and start afresh. The occupant would not be interested in the original appearance of the house he now lived in. He only asked himself if the total corresponded with his idea of how a house ought to look, and if it did not, he would attempt to improve it.[4]

It concerns the assessing and choosing of innumerable small details, the manifestation of preferences and whims. It concerns the freedom to know better than others, or to do the same as others. It has to do with the care to maintain, or the carelessness about private possessions, with the sudden urge to change as well as the stubborn desire to conserve and keep. It is related to the need to display and to create one's own environment, but also the desire to share that of others, or to follow a fashion. The need to give one's personal stamp is as important as the inclination to be unobtrusive. In short, it all has to do with the need for a personal environment where one can do as one likes; indeed it concerns one of the strongest urges of mankind: the desire for possession.[5]

Choice and Control

The builder-developer has dehumanized the housing consumer. Row after row of identical blocks, identical units, identical living rooms are suited for automatons, not people. No better environment has ever existed for a totalitarian state. Variations are superficial and cosmetic in nature. These projects, be they public housing or middle-class homes, are equally sterile, and the disadvantages are so familiar that we need not dwell on them here. Small wonder that the so-called counterculture and numerous other malcontent subcultures prefer the older neighborhoods. Alternate lifestyles can hardly emerge in newly constructed, yet deprived environments.

Deprived environments as used here means places that are lacking in physical facilities and opportunities for social interaction and that are limited in aesthetic satisfaction and environmental experience. Everything may well be new and clean, but the place has little to capture and hold the interest of adults and children alike. In short, such environments do not have an

Figure 1-8
A manifestation of possession. Note: This small house in Eugene, Oregon, was remodelled by a young couple. It had no porch and the few small openings looked out on a bare front yard. The result may not necessarily coincide with everyone's dream home, but the place conveys an image that the owners can identify with. They obviously took pride in detailing the posts and skylights.

absorbing and engaging character (Figures 1-9 and 1-10).

The test of any residential architecture may well be: Will it be supportive of significant variations in lifestyles, and more importantly, will it promote rather than impede the ascent of man? Will it permit him to externalize his existence, will it further a more humane life, or will it exert its brutal and degrading leveling force on society?

People with extreme lifestyles may well need to go off by themselves where they do not threaten neighbors, but the ability on the part of the architecture to absorb departures from the norm does constitute a measure of success. The arguments between environmental determinists and those professing no influence of the environment on man go on. The concept of dialectics remains foreign to the design disciplines.

Externalization of one's existence may occasionally result in houses painted red with turquoise trim

or similar expressions, and it may well be that the community must establish standards that do not affront the inhabitants sensibilities. To externalize, however, means to give material expression to existence. It does not just concern the exterior of our dwellings, but every aspect of us and our surround-

Figure 1-9
Apartment buildings in Eugene, Oregon. Note: These structures may be considered an example of a deprived environment. The windows shown facing each other provide the primary view since the windows at the opposite end of the apartments look into the corridors. The curtains are always drawn at both ends of the apartments, and no one has ever been seen on the roof at left.

Figure 1-10
An apartment building in Manhattan, Kansas. Note: There are thousands of apartments similar to this example of a deprived environment everywhere. The building sits as an object in a parking lot. The fake mansard roof and the token balconies, used for ubiquitous barbecues and little else, are cosmetic embellishments to disguise the aesthetic and experiential poverty of the place.

ings: our clothing, possessions, cars, and the nature of our gardens. Through externalization, we communicate our tastes, preferences, and status in life.

Today the nature of the housing development is decided by experts, and this decision is handed down from above. People can only contribute lip service to the planning process: "We could play at the game of citizen participation so long as participation was limited to amelioration."[6] The community is rarely given a choice between one type of building or another, between high-rise towers or high-density habitats. At most, local groups have been able to stop undesirable projects, such as freeways, from destroying their neighborhoods. Here and there renovation of what exists has replaced proposed new construction.

Generally, however, the community has not been able to influence design decisions. In the name of economy, it has to settle for housing that is hopelessly inadequate and already obsolete when occupied. The means seldom determine the quality of the environment; imagination and a quest for excellence do. These are abilities too rare even among the design professions. Projects are seldom awarded on the basis of design quality. Commissions are landed through extensive connections, lobbying, or having political muscle. The public, be it a neighborhood group or a future tenant looking for an apartment, has no say in the choice, short of not renting at all.

As should be quite apparent by now, architects under the present setup, even with the best of intentions, have not been effective in improving the lot of housing occupants. Another approach is needed.

If we are to avoid regimentation and create a human environment with potential for alternate futures, control of some of this environment must be returned to users. This control will need to be exercised in at least two scales: community scale and unit scale. Control on the community scale will have to be realized through public insistence on and approval of the best possible housing proposal under the circumstances. Such community control is no different from any other call for public involvement.

THE TOWNFRAME

Housing control on the community scale involves the product and the degree of completion of that product. Instead of being responsible for completed dwelling environments, the architect as well as the

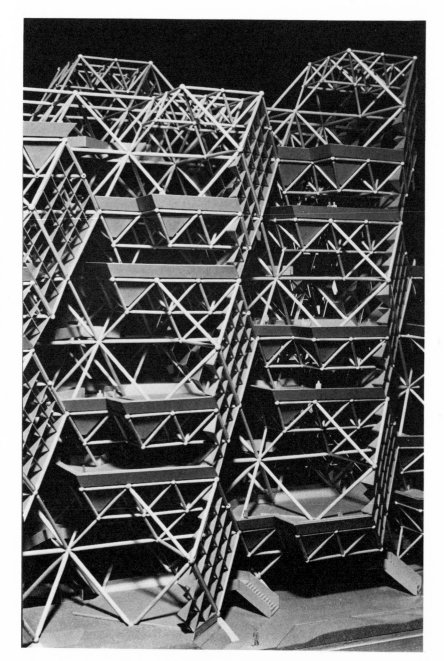

Figure 1–11
A multistory framework from the southeast. Note: This framework contains purchasable space lots ranging in size from one-story to three-story volumes with outdoor garden terraces and "landscape modules" (the inverted pyramidal containers for planting of small trees). The brise-soleil-type screens are privacy barriers between the space lots. The framework shows all the given systems except the built-in fireplace flues.

reviewing authority would confine their roles to design and assessment, respectively, of an "incomplete" framework and the plan for the whole development. This "townframe"[7] would consist of a physical structure, public access, infrastructure, and communal support facilities. In essence, it would constitute improvements on land suitable for individual dwellings (Figures 1-11 and 1-12). The townframe defines the limits of growth just like streets, sewers, power lines, and other utilities in an ordinary subdivision. Such environments can then grow to their physical saturation point and legal boundaries.

Control on the unit scale can then be left to the users—as though they were homeowners. The owner or long-term leaser of what could appropriately be called a space lot[8] within a framework would exercise his prerogatives. The "infil" in turn would have to conform to codes and additional established safety rules and be confined to the limits of individual property. Infil as used here refers to the small-scale construction within the framework for purpose of building the actual dwellings, shops, and so forth.

The framework can be designed to accept a high-technology infil system. The infil may fit the needs of one particular townframe, or it may be applicable to many other townframes. It can be produced to considerable sophistication by using the latest industrialized production methods with allowances for user manipulation. Its realization will require a considerable amount of imagination, design energy, and

Figure 1-12
A view from the southeast of a simulated user-completed framework. Note: This structure (scale: 1/2" = 1' 0") was assembled by architectural design students at the University of Oregon and then became the context for their design projects. No joint decisions were made on the nature of the infil system. Most proposals suggest current on-site construction; yet the individual designs are remarkably consistent, thereby conveying an emerging vernacular. The model shown in Figure 1-11 did not exist at this time, and the privacy screens had not been designed. (University of Oregon, 1974.)

expenditure. The unpredictable market, required volume of production, and the initial capital investment have plagued prefabricated housing schemes in the past and would likewise affect this approach. This option is an obvious and perpetually tempting one that is perhaps of greatest appeal to professionals. It has been advocated by Habraken[9] and others; yet the likelihood of its implementation remains as remote as ever.

The framework can be designed to accept an infinite number of high-technology, mutually related infil systems as well as handicraft substitutes and personal modifications. While this goal may well be the ultimate in housing design, it is unattainable in the near future. Its existence is dependent on standardization of space, a large market, and sophistication in the building industry. Existence of frameworks could be instrumental in bringing about such standardization. This alternative would conceptually go beyond the Japanese house, which permitted arranging, with some personalization, of a single system. People are innovative and will find ways of adapting industrialized components.

The framework can be filled in using present-day building methods of varying sophistication. The community may want to establish some standards in materials and finishes (as in the Sea Ranch, for example), or it may leave this choice up to the individual users. The architect, or for that matter the developer-builder, may provide built model dwellings and a design service ranging from free advice to a complete design and construction contract. This option makes possible testing the feasibility of user-completed frameworks immediately, as they are not dependent on investment in new technology.

The framework can be filled in in any conceivable way provided it does not create a hazard to neighboring lots. Such infil could range from tarpaper shacks and tents with outhouses to concrete block dwellings, mobile homes, and space truss greenhouses. This op-

tion is particularly applicable to housing problems of developing countries, since native building skills and materials could be used. Essentially no different from the squatter building process or so called alternatives in the industrialized West, the framework may well become the prevailing high-density building type. It could be designed to reinforce indigenous communal patterns. This approach could also be tested immediately anywhere, although it may well be transitory due to the continuous efforts of the inhabitants to upgrade their dwellings.

Granted, most people in the United States are unable, unprepared, and unwilling to build their own houses. Urban and to a large degree suburban and rural construction practices have divorced man from the building process. Opportunities for participation are most limited, and initiative is discouraged where most essential—that is, in public and other mass housing projects: ". . . when you live in a society with few incentives to develop skills for designing your own environment, you simply don't develop these skills."[10] Nevertheless, the opportunity and the right to decide the nature of one's dwelling should exist. After all, the owner of such a space lot can still ask a contractor to fill it in, or builders may provide ready-made houses, if that is what people really want.

Since the summer of 1975 the average American family can no longer afford to purchase a house. Increased leisure time and skyrocketing building costs may well prompt more and more people to do their own construction and so to become more intimately attached to their own dwelling. Such building also tends to result in a sharing of skills, thus fostering communal spirit:

. . . emphasis on people's ability to make environmental decisions should not be confused with a vision of a preindustrial, crafts-producing society with everybody building his own little house. While I and other architects find ourselves working at the level of handicrafts today (for lack of an appropriate technology to meet people's needs), that level of producing environment seems to me unnecessary and often undesirable.[11]

The long-range goal, nevertheless, should be some kind of user-manipulable system, as stated earlier. Whatever form building takes, be it arranging, erecting, modifying, or decorating, one's accomplishments are readily apparent. Creative building is a most satisfying activity, for building is living.

There will be objections and outcries from the elitists among the professions that such an environment will be disasterous and detrimental to the well-being of the inhabitants. In some cases that could be so, but then so is the present condition. Some inhabitants are likely to end up with dwellings that are ugly, "immoral," insensitive, or nonfunctional. However, this type of consequence could be called man's inherent right to be wrong. What is judged inappropriate by the professional is, after all, the product of the user who put his heart into it. Support of such freedom of choice is the very purpose of the framework. In an increasingly programmed society, allowances must be made for the unprogrammable and absurd. Only in a totalitarian state the "useless" is not permitted to exist.

2

Townframes versus Megastructures

We are spellbound by an anthill, a beehive, or the coral polyp edifices (Figure 2-1). Their social organizations, technological achievements, and environmental adaptation confront and challenge us. We may likely question our own accomplishments and find them wanting or, indeed, suicidal by comparison to other life forms.

Likewise, the Mesa Verde cliff dwellings, Dogon villages, Mediterranean hill towns, the high-rise clay towns in South Yemen (Figure 2-2), and other indigenous human settlements produce similar fascination. Yet seldom do our current urban environments give us comparable sensations.

The common focus of this attraction may well be evidence of the forces and processes that brought such an environment about and the signs of once present or ongoing life—life in its uncompromising, unremitting, often unconscious explicitness. The complex social structure necessary for its sustenance is readily discernible. In human settlements the connection between the environment and culture manifests itself through such physical evidence as buildings, possessions, land formations, art, and other remains. Construction is a visible reminder of the often pre-

Figure 2-1
Detail of cauliflower mushroom (*sparassis radicata*). Note: This rare mushroom may reach three to five feet in diameter in the Pacific Northwest. Its spatial complexity, structural capability, and "construction" process cannot be matched by manmade architecture. With little effort we can imagine ourselves in place of the little bugs that inhabit the mushroom and thus experience this environment from within. What a mind expanding sensation if we could really be in this architecture!

carious relationship between man and natural forces, in which human life is in a delicate balance and is continuously threatened with extinction.

Confrontation with the World Trade Center, the Pentagon, and similar megabuildings terminates in abhorrence. The convenient culprit is the lack of "human scale"—a label equally familiar to the architect and the layman—rather than the quality of these buildings. Although size and certainly height is a factor in our rejection of such buildings, the phenomenon is much more complex. These structures become synonymous with their tenants: the corporate establishment and the military complex. In many ways these are unfortunate buildings, but much of the fear, rejection, and hostility directed towards the tenants is transferred to the container. The now-demolished Les Halles Centrales of Paris was a megascale structure; yet its loss is lamented. The Chinese wall is the only man-built element visible from the moon (Figure 2–3). It has not failed to amaze man. As a construction feat, it remains unsurpassed for its size. The cultural and historical events and associations triggered by its existence are awe inspiring.

Could it be that we associate glass-enclosed superblocks with the mindless scurrying of the ant population and that we not only resent comparing ourselves with such predetermined lives but fear being caught in a similar coded existence? There is little in the way that these structures are designed and articulated to mitigate our anxieties. Thus the natural and human anthills (Figure 2–4) are at once hypnotic attractions and threatening reminders of ever-possible slavery. Yet the anonymous and repetitive glass-clad blocks and hill-town habitats are at opposite ends on the acceptance scale. Consequently, differentiation and analysis of megascale human environments are necessary.

DEFINING ELEMENTS OF THE MEGASCALE ENVIRONMENT

Hitherto all large buildings and building complexes have been called megastructures. *Progressive Architecture* has introduced the term *omnibuildings*[1] to emphasize their comprehensiveness. Further breakdown of various megascale human settlements is needed at this time.

A *megabuilding* is a very large building for housing one or only a few functions. It is a blown up version of any isolated "ordinary" building. There is no definite boundary between a large building and a megabuilding. Its impact on the environment may be considerable due to shadow, amount of space taken up by parking, traffic generated, services required, energy consumed, visual bulk, and so forth. Its psychological effect on people may be overbearing. Interior work spaces are likely to result in loss of contact with the environment, and the mass of humanity contained by it can hardly develop a sense of community. Chicago's Sears Tower and, once again, the Pentagon are megabuildings. Throughout history such buildings were built to communicate power and to impress the populace. The pyramids, St. Peter's Basilica, and Todaiji Daibutsuden are convenient examples of built manifestations of power (Figure 2–5).

On the positive side, megabuildings may shelter activities often precluded by the elements. Just because the super-domed stadia (Figure 2–6) have raised rather than resolved design problems, does not neces-

Figure 2-2
A view of Hadramaut, South Yemen. Note: The high-rise clay buildings, built primarily of the only available local material, are closely spaced to protect the inhabitants from the extreme heat and cold and from attacks by hostile tribes. Menacing and forbidding, yet haunting, such places exert their hypnotic influence on use. (After a photograph by Helen Keiser.)

sarily mean that the potential for humanly acceptable environment is not there. Megabuildings present a design challenge that invites serious response by architects and planners. The Vertical Assembly Building at the Kennedy Space Center is a megabuilding with its own interior weather—it rains within the megaspace.

A *megastructure* is a very large complex designed to support human activities of transitory nature—that is, a complex whose form is primarily determined by experiential factors and time-use cycles as well as structural and technical possibilities. The term has been used in its broadest sense to denote all of man's megascale building endeavors. Such structures have evolved in response to superscale building tasks like the freeway interchanges and bridges. Advances in structural systems have made possible enclosing vast volumes like Kenzo Tange's "Theme Center" for Expo '70 in Osaka and Frei Otto's tents for the

Figure 2–3 (above)
A view of the Great Wall of China at Nankow Pass. Note: The Chinese wall is the only man-built element on earth that is visible from the moon. It is 1,255 miles long if measured in a straight line and over 1,500 miles with its sinuosities. Twenty-five feet wide at the base and fifteen feet at the top, it varies in height from fifteen to thirty feet. The wall is punctuated with 25,000 towers. Started in 214 B.C. by Shih Hwang Ti, it was completed and reconstructed by the Ming Emperors in the fifteenth and sixteenth centuries and proved to be an ineffectual barrier against the Tartar and Mongol hordes. The Great Wall is the world's longest cemetary with bodies of dead or inefficient laborers crushed in the foundations. Chinese convicted by Emperor Shih Hwang Ti of having books in their possession constituted some of the forced labor.

Figure 2–4 (at right)
Taos Pueblo in New Mexico. Note: The indigenous building form of the Pueblo Indians seems to grow out of the earth. Such high-density housing is arranged around one or more courtyards and built out of mud plastered adobe—literally the stuff of earth. The terraced complex is the result of a cumulative building process that reflects the changing needs of the clan. Dilapidated rooms are demolished and new sections are added. The human anthill is shaped by the communal social structure and religious rites as much as by the available materials, climate, and the economic basis of existence. (Photograph by Robert Miller, Eugene, Oregon.)

Figure 2-5
Todaiji Daibutsuden, the Hall of the Great Buddha in Nara, Japan. Note: This temple was completed in 751 to promote Buddhism as the state religion. Daibutsuden houses a 53' high bronze Buddha. Originally 11 by 7 bays, it measured 290' by 170' and 163' high, including the 11' stone base. It was burned to the ground in 1180 and rebuilt in 1190 and then burned again in 1567. The present version was completed in 1708 only at two-thirds its original size (188' by 166' and 157' high). The lower roof cantilevers almost 30'. It is the largest wood building in the world.

Munich Olympics and similar projects since the Crystal Palace (Figure 2-7).

Although application of such structures to housing or centers of leisure is often based on technical possibilities, the ultimate impact is social. The convergence of human activities is what has given impetus to the megastructure movement.

The log-like office building configurations in Tange's Plan for Tokyo Bay and his Tsukiji Project (Figure 2-8) may be among the more promising schemes. These have been widely copied, but only the image rather than a genuine megastructure was built at Kofu in Japan (Figure 2-9). Such proposals approach city size and their impact should not be minimized. They do, however, begin to recognize the continuity of the built environment. Response to the complexity of human existence should make these

projects less stark and include the often missing humanizing support systems.

It is not so much size that characterizes megastructures, but the long-term nature of the framework and the short-term aspect of the infil units. These may, in fact, be "plugged-in" like the stunning Plug-In City project by Peter Cook of Archigram (1963–64), a project which galvanized a decade[2] and changed the direction of the movement. The drawings brought together many of the images employed by the megastructure collective at the time. The "Man the Producer" theme pavilion for Expo '67 was also designed and built during this period (1964–1966) (Figures 2-10, 2-11, and 2-35).

The work of Renzo Piano and Richard Rogers complete this period in the development of megastructures. Centre Pompidou in Paris (Figures 2-12 and 2-13) is the ultimate monument to the flexible leisure complex and the most Archigrammatic example built.

A *megaenvironment* is a very large manmade facility generally designed for a limited purpose in which the components cannot be divorced from their context. The megaenvironment is an integrated one (Figure 2-14). Buildings, entertainment structures, airplane approach ramps, vehicular or pedestrian circulation networks, land forms, or other features are characterized by their inability to exist independent of each other. Form is the result of not only the needs of each component but the relationship between the parts to the whole. These are highly desirable attributes. Separated from their context, the buildings may appear even more awkward than usual. The difference is one of degree rather than kind. Unfortunately, neither society nor its representatives have used this approach to affect day-to-day living significantly. Few new town developments attempt to integrate their facilities in a comparable way.

The Dallas–Fort Worth Regional Airport and Disneyland are megaenvironments. World's fairs and

Figure 2-6
The King County super-domed stadium in Seattle. Note: Surrounded by parking lots and lacking in scale-giving elements, the dome is not an inviting building to approach. People are overpowered by cars and intimidated by the size of the structure. Landscaping and higher level covered pedestrian approachways with supporting services could have provided the transition between this megabuilding and the urban circulation systems.

Olympic Games sites are also megaenvironments, and they even contain megabuildings like the Contemporary Resort Hotel in the Florida Disney World. Their very existence to a large degree is a reflection of social values, and society pays a high price for such centers of entertainment. There may well be an

(Text continued on page 23.)

Figure 2-7 (at right)
Sir Joseph Paxton's The Crystal Palace. Note: The construction of this building marked a radical departure in the history of building. Designed for The Great London Exhibition of 1851, it set the course of exhibitions for almost a century throughout the world. A marvel of the Victorian period, it ushered in a revolutionary approach to building. Few modern industrialization techniques can match Paxton's innovations. Designed and built in about six months, this megastructure is 1,851 feet long. (From a lithograph, source unknown.)

Figure 2-8

A plan for the Tokyo Tsukiji Area by Kenzo Tange and URTEC (1967). Note: This scheme, which is based on a 1960 plan for Tokyo, does away with the distinction between the city and the buildings. The city is a huge space grid rather than a collection of isolated individual buildings. The system, its components, and the frequency and limits of expansion become more important than the form, which, by implication, is never complete. (Photograph courtesy of Osamu Murai, ©, Tokyo, Japan.)

Figure 2–8
A plan for the Tokyo Tsukiji Area by Kenzo Tange and URTEC (1967). Note: This scheme, which is based on a 1960 plan for Tokyo, does away with the distinction be-tween the city and the buildings. The city is a huge space grid rather than a collection of isolated individual buildings. The system, its components, and the frequency and limits of expansion become more important than the form, which, by implication, is never complete. (Photograph courtesy of Osamu Murai, ©, Tokyo, Japan.)

Figure 2-9
Kenzo Tange's (with URTEC) Yamanashi Communications Centre (1966) at Kofu in Japan. Note: This design conveys the image of a megastructure without fully exploiting its potential. The voids between the circular cores communicate expansion within the grid defined by these cores. The towers, too closely spaced, house a multitude of functions, which thus obscures their role as vertical circulation carriers. Although beam ends suggest dismantling and additions, the structure and the conventional construction do not facilitate such changes. Thus Tange's only built "megastructure" is simply a monument to adaptability and expansion—an illusion of a megastructure. (Photograph courtesy of Japan Architect Co., Ltd, ©, Tokyo, Japan.)

Figure 2-10
"Man the Producer" theme pavilion of Expo '67 in Montreal by Affleck, Desbarats, Dimakopoulos, Lebensold, and Sise, Architects. Note: The exhibition megastructure spans a canal
and major pedestrian and vehicular routes and houses a number of subtheme exhibits of
scientific nature.

Figure 2-11 (at left)
The truncated tetrahedral space at the west end of the "Man the Producer" pavilion. Note: A fully automated factory penetrates several floors of this space in the pavilion, which has been called an exhibition in itself. Conceived as a spatial system and an environmental experience, it is the most ambitious space truss structure ever built.

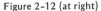

Figure 2-12 (at right)
West side of Centre Pompidou, Paris, by Renzo Piano and Richard Rogers. Note: Conceived as a flexible matrix for participatory entertaining environmental experience, the building now houses the national collection of modern art, a library, lecture halls, a restaurant, children's art classrooms, a day-care center/library and other fixed facilities. The result of an international competition, the centre was completed in 1977 and still succeeds in conveying the image of a megastructure. People on the enclosed yet exposed escalators animate this west side and various events manage, at times, to fill the barren plaza. Although the structure does not contain transitory functions and its size is well exceeded by many old or new buildings, the explicitness of all systems and the absence of self-conscious formalism communicate the spirit and intent of a megastructure.

Figure 2–13
East facade of Centre Pompidou, Paris, by Renzo Piano and Richard Rogers. Note: The exposed pipes, ducts, and other mechanical systems of this east facade blend in well with the old buildings.

ingrained need for such escapes and dream worlds. The very name "dreamland" has become a generic description of such complexes in Japan.[3]

An *omnibuilding* is a building for housing a large variety of human needs. Omnibuildings need not necessarily be very large as they are characterized by diversity and self-sufficiency. *Progressive Architecture* has labelled the pre-industrial peasant house a mini-omnibuilding.[4] Contemporary omnibuildings, however, are likely to be rather large due to the demands of modern life and specialization in production and service. Unlike a megabuilding, it includes as many of the facilities essential to daily life as possible. Restaurants and shops tend to conglomerate in mega-buildings due to their large size and the difficulty of going elsewhere for such services. In omnibuildings supporting functions are integrated from the outset in recognition of their interdependence and the inevitable need of self-sufficiency. Some recent built examples have emerged. Montreal's Place Bonaventure (Figure 2–15) with its train and subway stations, parking, retail shops, cinema, exhibition and merchandizing floors, hotel and gardens may come closest to fitting this label, although it does not integrate housing and civic institutions, nor any production facilities. Chicago's John Hancock building also fits this definition. It contains apartments, offices, parking, restaurants and an assortment of supporting shops and services. In the case of the latter, it is difficult to justify sub-jugation of diverse functions to the tapering form and the structural demands of the high-rise. Omnibuildings rather than omnistructures may be best suited for hostile environments, and indeed there are a number

Figure 2–14
A pleasure palace by Li Yung-Chin (Yuan dynasty). Note: The pavilions and courtyards in this Chinese painting seem to grow out of the landscape. This manmade counterpart to the distant mountains creates a meandering megaenvironment of sumptuous complexity. (Collection of the National Palace Museum, Taipei, Taiwan, Republic of China.)

Figure 2-15
Place Bonaventure in Montreal. Note: This seventeen-story high superblock is built on Canadian National Railway air rights. It is a milestone in urban development in size, but, more importantly, in its attempt to integrate the diversity of facilities. (Affleck, Desbarats, Dimakopoulos, Lebensold, and Sise, Architects.)

of proposals for habitats beyond the Arctic Circle and over oceans. The city itself may be viewed with apprehension by the residents who see little reason to leave their enclave. The tenants of the Hancock building enjoy spectacular views and sunsets and must check with the building's weather report about the climate at street level. Paolo Soleri's arcologies are extreme examples of omnibuildings on a city scale.

An *omnistructure* is a very large complex for housing a variety of human needs whose form is primarily determined by these needs rather than structural pos-

sibilities. Magazines abound with bridge-type megastructures filled with housing units. An omnistructure is not preconditioned by such rigid technological determinants. Like an omnibuilding, the ultimate omnistructure is a self-contained environment not unlike a small city. It may consist of a collection of buildings or an extremely meandering continuum together with access systems and landscaping much like that of megaenvironments. The difference lies in its comprehensiveness versus the special-use orientation of megaenvironments.

Contrary to many claims by architectural periodicals, no convincing contemporary omnistructures have been built. Frequently cited examples, such as the town center of Cumbernauld new town in Scotland, are still primarily shopping centers. Cumbernauld and the emerging mixed-use buildings are precursors of omnistructures.

The best examples of omnistructures may well be medieval monasteries such as Cluny III or Clairvaux (Figure 2-16), just to name two of the more complex from among the many.[5] Some of the more self-sufficient castles could likewise qualify as omnistructures.

A *townframe* is a large three-dimensional structure, a matrix for housing human needs, and an all-encompassing spatial modulator and facilitator. A townframe is the ultimate megastructure. It is a hierarchy of systems necessary for the support of the complexity of man's existence. In its most complete state it may shelter the whole range of activities: home life, work, play, study, and contemplation. It consists of a structural framework, an infrastructure of three-dimensional service networks, communication and transportation systems, and an array of served volumes. A city relies on two-dimensional land use. A townframe integrates diverse facilities three dimensionally. Such townframes are inevitable answers to the dilemma of two-dimensional land use and ensuing urban sprawl. A townframe recognizes and facilitates three-dimensional transformation of the urban fabric. It is the logical container of omni- or megastructures, housing neighborhoods, or city cores. Three-dimensional land use is dependent on physical or conceptual townframe.

No townframes have been built. The more imaginative proposals, like Yona Friedman's "Spatial Town"[6] schemes (Figures 2-17 and 2-18) or the proposals by Eckhard Schulze-Fielitz, remain in the conceptual stage.

No other building concept holds as much promise and versatility for the urbanizing world. Inevitably, an interconnected Montreal or Minneapolis (Figures

2-19 and 2-20) would be representative of a set of functions and values quite different from a communal townframe in the Oregon woods on a village scale or a settlement in the Philippines. The means of livelihood, lifestyle, and the environment will shape each omnistructure and townframe. The degree to which these townframes will remain supportive as well as able to undergo transformation short of destruction will be their measure of success.

VISIONARY PROJECTS

Numerous so-called visionary projects have resulted only in self-serving statements hardly contributive to architecture. Conceptual proposals may be of value in image formation, but the frequency of their appearance discredits the design professions. The layman quite justifiably suspects that the majority of these megastructures cannot be realized, or if indeed built, they may well jeopardize what little there remains of a human environment. As a consequence, the very

(Text continued on page 29.)

Figure 2-16
Detail of the monastery Clairvaux plan by Milley (1708 engraving by C. Lukas). Note: This English Benedictine monastery and originally a small Cistercian church, like others of its era, provides an example of omnistructures. In 1115 Abbot Bernard started an expansion and construction program for Clairvaux. The 2,870 yard-long wall encloses a refectory, cloisters, novitiate, and many other functions as well as a myriad arrangement of ancillary buildings for craftsmen, guests, and a sick-zone. It was a prototype for many other monasteries of the order. The complex had its own water supply and a plan for expansion. There were buildings for every craft and art providing for the earthly needs of monastic life. The monastery was destroyed during the French Revolution. See Wolfgang Braunfels, *Monasteries of Western Europe*, Alastair Laing, translated (Princeton, N.J.: Princeton University Press, 1972).

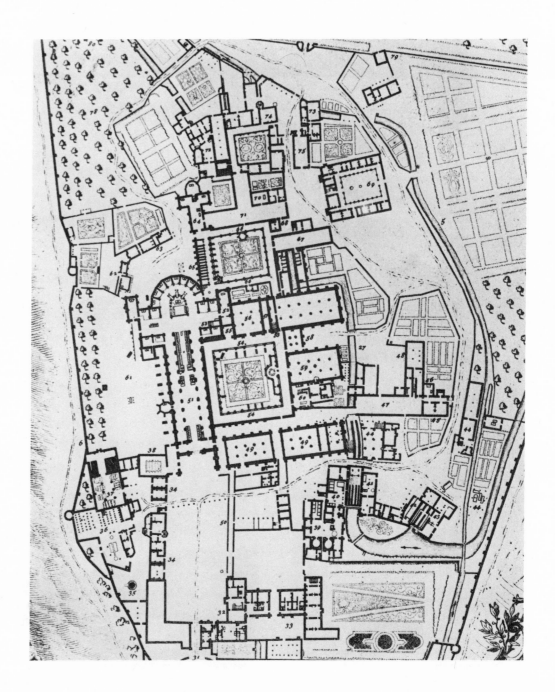

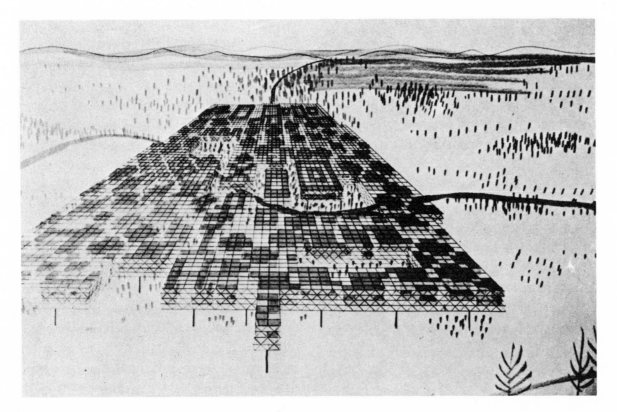

Figure 2–17 (at left)
Yona Friedman's proposal for an ever-changing society. Note: This proposed "Spatial Town" is a matrix for changing needs. It provides for three-dimensional town planning and flexibility in space utilization. (Reprinted with permission from Verlag Gerd Hatje GMBH, Stuttgart; from Justus Dahinden, *Urban Structures for the Future* [New York: Praeger, 1972].)

Figure 2–18 (at right)
Friedman's proposed "Spatial Town" over Paris. Note: Friedman has suggested building over cities and phased rebuilding of cities, but his proposals have not been developed during the past two decades. Although there are obvious problems, such as light to buildings below, the proposal is revolutionary and responsible, yet unconvincing to all but a few. (Reprinted with permission from Verlag Gerd Hatje GMBH, Stuttgart; from Justus Dahinden, *Urban Structures for the Future* [New York: Praeger, 1972].)

Figure 2-20 (at right)
A corrective measure for an obsolete urban environment.
Note: The Minneapolis Skyway System is an attempt by
the Minneapolis Planning and Development Department
to revitalize the downtown and to respond to the frigid
weather. Although the links are changing the use of some of
the second floors of the city buildings, the nature of the
network is limited by the existing structure.

Figure 2-19 (at left)
A view of the Minneapolis Skyway System next to Philip
Johnson's IDS Building. Note: This system will connect
fifty-four blocks of the central city by 1985. With more
than a dozen of the sixty-four planned skyways already
in existence, the city is taking on a third dimension in its
pedestrian circulation.

Figure 2–21

"The Tower of Babel," by Peter Bruegel the Elder. Note: Bruegel's painting depicts the construction of the enormous tower in the Flemish landscape, and a similar painting shows the tower in its finished state. The awesome undertaking and size is all too apparent, yet it is undeniably fascinating. Does it not respond to our collective consciousness? (Kunsthistorisches Museum, Vienna.)

term *megastructure* conjures up monstrous visions in the spirit of Fritz Lang's film *Metropolis*, despite the fact that megascale buildings have been with us since antiquity. The pyramids and the towers of Babel still fire man's imagination (Figure 2-21).

Unless we take pains to push these proposals beyond the conceptual, they will continue to lack credibility. This arduous task is absolutely essential in assessing the nature of such environments and the role of the inhabitants and other users. Yona Friedman's proposal for building within a space truss spanning over Paris remains as unconvincing as to the livability within it or its impact on the environment below as when it was first suggested some two decades ago.[7] He has not been willing or able to develop it much beyond the early sketches and computer models.

Many of the utopian proposals of megascale proportions address themselves to the transitory nature of industrialized societies and the taken-for-granted cornucopia of consumer culture. These proposals employ anticipatory technology and are characterized by a mechanistic aesthetic. The graphics of the Archigram group (Figure 2-22) are representative of this trend. Everyone is "turned-on, tuned-in, and hip." There is an abundance of sensory stimulation and immediate gratification of needs. Only the young and the beautiful inhabit these future pleasure structures. As pointed out by Manfredi Nicoletti, these idealized yet often seductively appealing designs share a basic deficiency in their refusal to go beyond the conceptual stage.[8] Thus, their contribution is extremely limited: They identify an alternative present (rather than future).

The future cannot be anticipated in design. If building a structure at all is possible, it can be built at the time of conception. Louis Kahn said:

. . . if you know what a thing will look like fifty years from now, you can do it now. But you don't know, because the way that a thing will be fifty years from now is what it will be. There are certain natures which will always be true.[9]

The process of concretization transforms such conceptual images beyond recognition. Conflicting situations have to be resolved, sizes adjusted, and relationships changed. Structures that depend on some magic future material will never be built. Such materials, when they do appear, exert their own demands beyond the imagination of earlier times and evolve new forms and methods inconceivable by the most gifted just a decade or so before. Discoveries and innovations in structure systems have brought about tent, pneumatic, cable, and space truss structures resulting in forms unanticipated by any futurist.

Almost any shape can be built provided one finds the appropriate corrective measures. The majority of Soleri's proposals (see, for example, Figure 2-24) can be realized only at a great cost to society in terms of resource depletion and energy consumption. Cer-

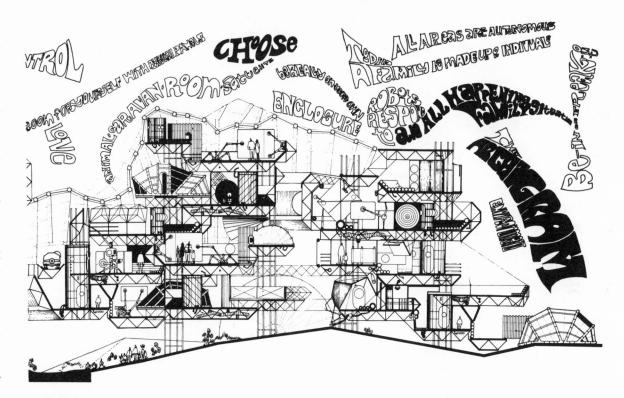

Figure 2-22
Cartoon-like detail section of "control-and-choice" project by Peter Cook, Dennis Crompton, and Ron Herron with graphics by Warren Chalk. Note: The drawings of the Archigram group have been widely publicized and have resulted in an increased awareness of "plug-in" architecture. Influenced by the space program and dependent on dental chair and hair dryer type of gadgetry and baby carriage-like convertible enclosures, the mechanistic environments cater to a media-oriented mass society. (Reprinted with permission of Archigram.)

tainly, they would not get built without drastic changes.

Preoccupation with the technological side of mega- and omnistructures holds us back from focusing on the more crucial social and psychological implications of such environments that are the primary responsibility and opportunity of form givers. At their best, architects have articulated the noblest values and aspirations of society. Giving physical expression to the times is not enough. Worthy and, moreover, achievable models must alter the direction of humanity. We desperately need schemes—buildable today with existing technologies—that would permit assessment of their implied quality of life.

URBAN ENVIRONMENT AS A TOWNFRAME

In a broader interpretation the idea of townframes represents not only a highly complex physical "organism" but a way of looking at and interpreting the existing built environment. This interpretation signals an awareness of the relatedness of all systems. It recognizes that much in our urban environment constitutes a de facto omni- or megastructure. Acknowledgment of the existence of such ordering frameworks permits us to take full advantage of their implications.

The very existence of any part of our urban fabric depends on the infrastructure of utilities, communication networks, and spatial order. Few experts employed in its design, administration, construction, and maintenance profess awareness of the interrelatedness of these systems. The infrastructure of Manhattan or any other city defies human comprehension. Control over the physical systems and the ensuing corresponding bureaucracies is often on the verge of breakdown.

Even the infrastructure of single-family housing subdivisions remains incomprehensible to the homeowners. Not being aware of the magnitude and the role of each system, they are unlikely to express any interest in disposal problems or conservation measures. Only a sudden interruption of the service—a power failure, an overflowing sewer, or a broken water main—makes one aware of these lifelines. By hiding the power lines from our view, we eliminate them from our consciousness. Unconcern, abuse, and wastefulness are the likely consequences.

Much in the existing order is abstract. Setbacks, height restrictions, limits on amount and type of construction, zoning, and so forth represent legal rather than physical order. This order, despite the lack of visible limits, does result in a two- or three-dimensional perceivable environment. Some of these legal restrictions, such as setbacks, height of fences, and laws governing planting of trees, are difficult to understand and enforce if need be. These legal boundaries and regulations are not reinforced through explicit physical features. The street, sidewalk, and the planting strip between are clearly demarked. Any infringement would be noticeable and in direct conflict with public interest. The individual person understands this, and defiance is the exception rather than the rule. The urban environment is an implicit megascale omnistructure, an abstract two-dimensional townframe (Figure 2–23).

The order of a townframe is physical and explicit. It may be regular or irregular, continuous or discontinuous, but it is more or less explicit. This order is likely to be three-dimensional, and the spatial system may be defined by a general structural framework. Other space and use-defining elements, such as circulation networks and platforms for infil, are likely to be dominant features. The legal framework permits construction and change on ordinary building lots. In townframes this legal framework is an apparent general reference frame that facilitates conception and subsequent transformations of such built environments. This reference frame is not the result of an abstract quest for order, but is necessitated by the close proximity of the supported facilities and three-dimensional space planning. The life-supporting infrastructure likewise can no longer be completely hidden below ground. Explicit townframes recognize, or rather should recognize, the interdependence of all systems.

SYSTEMS VERSUS OBJECTS

How we view our environment would matter very little if it did not affect our lives and day-to-day experiences. An awareness that any addition or change in the urban structure has a bearing on all the other parts of the environment acknowledges the existence of the implicit townframe. An object-oriented attitude results in design of buildings as objects. On the other hand, realization that manmade environment consists of many mutually dependent systems, which in their interdependence are akin to and extensions of natural systems, may more likely terminate in design of whole places rather than unrelated parts. Such places constitute an ecology of built environment where the hard edge between building and landscape, interior and exterior, street and corridor, roof drain and irrigation ditch may be less harsh; buildings and their context become inseparable and inconceivable without each other.

The fallacy of many proposed omnibuildings such as Paolo Soleri's, regardless of their considerable positive qualities, is that they are form conscious rather than systems conscious (Figure 2–24). Once again we see a manifestation of our object-oriented thinking. The self-conscious thing is not only offensive, but through its size often overpowering. Individual control is inconceivable, and the identity of man appears threatened. Small wonder that we react negatively to any suggestion of a megastructure.

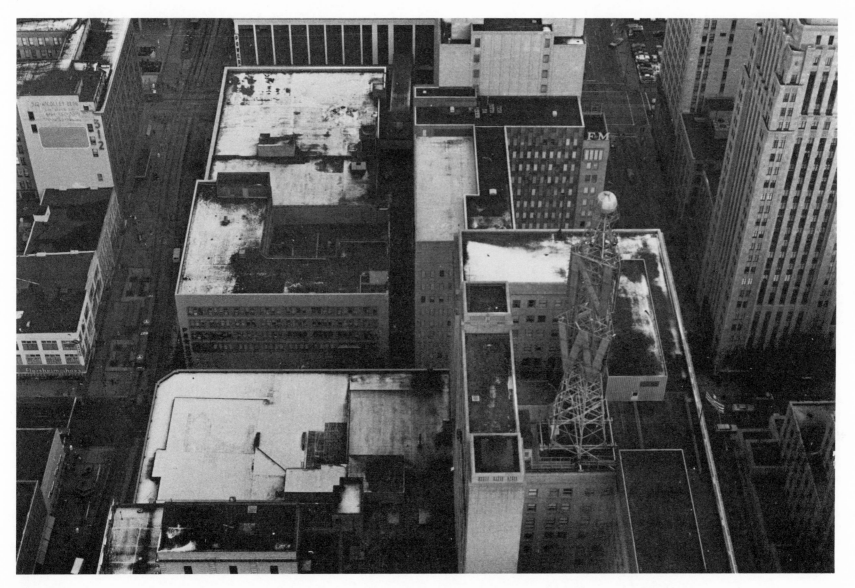

Figure 2–23
Minneapolis from above. Note: This view is an example of the city as an implicit omnistructure. Most buildings in urban contexts are no longer distinguished as individual objects. They are more or less closely integrated components of the urban fabric. Recognition of this phenomena should lead to design of explicit townframes and awareness of environmental, social, architectural, and other advantages.

TOWNFRAME AND GROWTH

In view of our building needs, large-scale projects will be with us for quite some time. If city and town planning were viewed as a three-dimensional endeavor, omnistructures and townframes could be a reality. Incremental growth would be divorced from mindless land-based sprawl and confined to the innards of a designed framework. The location and configuration of the townframe would be based on optimum available land for such settlements with agricultural land, forest and wildlife preserves, and ecologically sensitive areas set aside. Additive and forever-expanding land-consuming types of growth would then be replaced by an internal transformation, similar to the policy practiced by city dwellers in earlier times.

The macrostructure—that is, the townframe—can evolve incrementally just as the intrastructure does. An essential factor is, however, that this expansion follow a pattern of growth consistent with the characteristics of the macrostructure and in compliance with the land-use policies stated earlier. The traditional master-plan approach to planning is unrealistic; the plans hardly ever get carried out, thereby resulting too often in an urban wasteland. The promise of plans lies in the future; yet users live in the present. They are as much in need of a supportive environment as future generations. Piecemeal growth, on the other hand, is responsible for the current endless strip developments, the general detrimental nature of our urban environment, and suicidal speculative degradation of land and other resources. Lacking any organizing structure, laissez-faire expansion proceeds without the guidance and foresight of a plan. Street and utility layouts and zoning ordinances attempt to control the two-dimensional city. Zoning has not, however, been

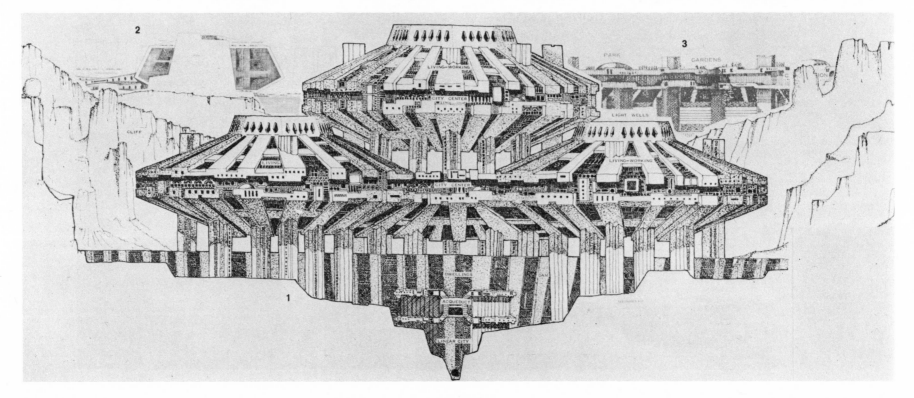

Figure 2-24
Elevation of Paolo Soleri's arcology ("architecture" plus "ecology") Babeldiga for a population of 1,200,000. Note: Two of the three Babels in this design bear directly into the dam stabilizing its structure. The forms are 1,400-2,100 meters high, resulting in close to six cubic kilometers of sheltered and shaded space. (Reprinted from *Arcology* by Paolo Soleri, by permission of the MIT Press, Cambridge, Mass.)

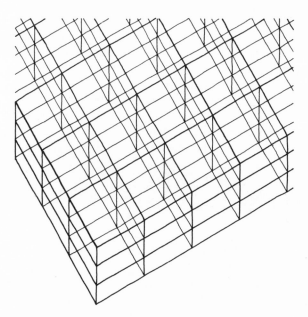

Figure 2-25
A simplistic, repetitious Miesian-type of modular system. Note: Such general uniform modules may be determined by structural feasibility, aesthetics, or construction requirements. They are, however, convincing only for anonymous, unspecified spaces and unpredictable or flexible uses. There is no differentiation between access ways, space required for life support systems, and the served volumes. Repetitious module systems have dominated modern architecture for decades and thus contributed to the general monotony of the built environment.

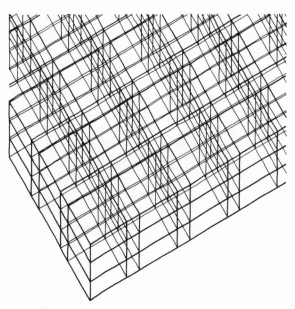

Figure 2-26
A sophisticated modular system. Note: Separation of identical volumes by an intermediate space implies spatial zoning. The narrow modules can be allocated to circulation networks, utilities, projections, or similar service uses, depending on the nature of the framework. The application is, of course, dependent on size and geometry. Such modular zoning can be further extended to recognize every system of the framework.

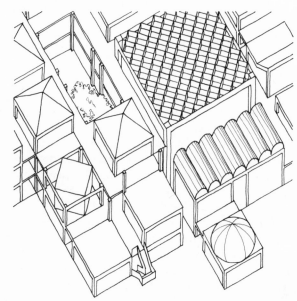

Figure 2-27
Application of the sophisticated modular system (shown in Figure 2-26). Note: More complex orders permit easy adaptation to particular use, such as articulation of spaces, zoning for access ways, transformation of structure due to larger spans, and so forth. Space function and expression can be more closely related than in the repetitious modular system.

an effective tool in structuring land use. It has been used to protect investments and to keep the poor in their place; yet real estate lobbies have discovered numerous methods for changing zoning to serve their own interests.[10]

Consequently, the rules of expansion of the three-dimensional city must be communicated or, better yet, dictated, by the macrostructure; advantages, if clearly visible, may prevent arbitrary departure from the initiated order. Access and life-support systems and the geometry of the townframe make up the clearest, most direct, and visible blueprint to this order, but this geometry must not generate a simplistic repetitious Miesian structure (Figure 2-25). Kahn's clarification "by order I do not mean orderliness"[11] expands on the nature of order. Perpetuating a uniform grid by fiat is increasingly difficult. Such frameworks may not be extended after the initial construction and the termination of the original designer's responsibilities.

There is no absolutely sure way that any plan of action will be followed short of dictatorial measures.

Survival of the fittest governs evolution in nature and guarantees continuity through propagation and continuous transformations and adaptations. Extension of the townframe does not appreciably differ from analogies in nature. If the geometry recognizes as many of the requirements for human existence as possible and achieves them with an economy of means, it is likely to expand. Inevitably, townframes will be considerably complex structures and their orders highly sophisticated (Figures 2-26, 2-27 and 5-20). Respect of cultural, environmental, social, and psychological forces will result in geometries that can communicate location and extent of occupiable spaces, access systems, open areas, voids, crucial relationships, and orientation. These are but a few of the demands on the order that render the abstract concrete and particular to the place (Figure 2-28). The geometry takes on meaning, and the varying volumes contain inherent clues on their intended use. The outmoded gridiron street pattern provides such clues in the two-dimensional city. Such order does not preclude future changes in additions to the framework; in fact, hopefully each addition would benefit and learn from the earlier and improve on it.

The framework must follow a master plan; yet be "complete" at each stage of its development. Instead of the current single-scale pattern of growth, incremental growth then would proceed simultaneously along two scales: the urban framework scale and the individual infil scale (Figure 2-29). The large anonymous megabuildings housing a collection of tenants could then be replaced by the ongoing townframe that would provide the necessary connections as well as recognize and articulate the identity of each element within. This goal may sound like a tall order, but it is entirely possible and feasible if the relationships between systems and subsystems are understood and the boundaries of responsibility defined.

No other building concept offers greater opportunities for phased incremental—and less-destructive—transformation of our existing cities. Many municipal utilities are badly in need of replacement: Circulation networks are saturated, buildings are dilapidated, and the land, due to two-dimensional expansion, is underutilized. If connections to existing urban systems are carefully considered, the supporting framework could be built in modest portions on randomly available parcels of land. They would then get extended or connected as additional land and capital became available and would incorporate latest changes learned from the initial designs. Some segments may be quite

modest, while others may never get connected. The framework would meander in response to available land, natural features, preservable sections of the city, architectural monuments, or whatever other reason (Figure 2-29). Such a structure sprouting among the isolated and disconnected buildings and parking lots would be organic in nature. The distinction between the city and the building would disappear. The imposed isolation between individual buildings would be

eliminated. Consequently, the townframe would less likely end up as a form-conscious megabuilding; the form would be the result of the numerous and contradictory social, economic, and natural forces. With the inherent capacity of the structure system and the utility infrastructure exercising a healthy restraint, design of such a townframe is never complete—its form reflects the dynamics of urban life.

The townframe approach does not imply continu-

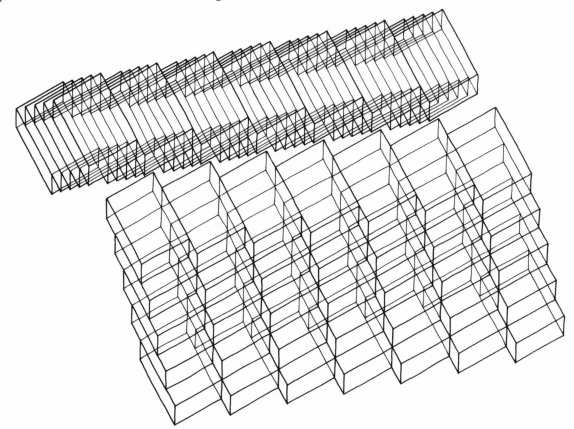

Figure 2-28
A framework with implied meaning. Note: The terraced modules suggest housing. Module systems can be designed to fulfill particular architectural goals. Too often, however, simplistic modules predetermine the resulting architecture.

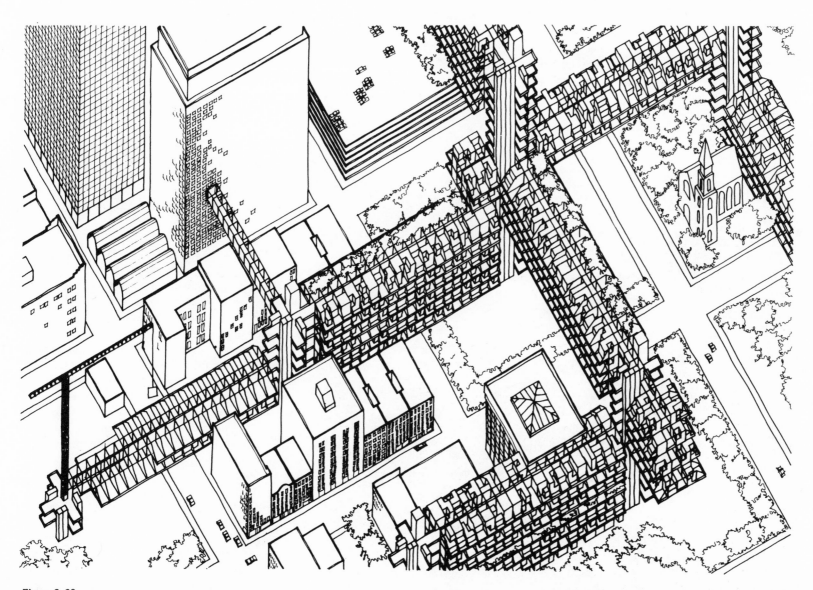

Figure 2-29
Incremental growth at two scales: the framework scale and the individual space-lot scale. Note: Such frameworks can be integrated with the existing structures or the method can be applied to phased rebuilding of dilapidated urban areas. By going over, between, or in place of existing buildings as suggested by Yona Friedman (Figure 2-18) and others, this approach to revitalizing inner-city areas would be the least disruptive renewal where restoration could not be justified. Changes within each space lot or, for that matter, larger volumes within the framework can go on throughout the duration of the structure.

ous expenditures any more than our current building-by-building approach. It does require reexamination of land ownership and methods of land acquisition. The real costs of present urban sprawl are hidden. Transformation of existing cities would permit simultaneous repair of neighborhoods. We would be in error to consider phased building of the townframe as a public matrix for individualism and withdrawal or conversely as an instrument for homogeneity. Mass housing is the most extreme application of orderliness; yet cities traditionally did reflect the complexity and individual accommodations in a restrained environment.

There is little doubt at this time that such frameworks would be ecologically least damaging to the natural environment from all the options (short of population control) open to man. The prospects of a stable world population are dim. United Nations figures indicate a doubling of world population in the next thirty years. Nearly all of the additional 3,500 million people will live in towns and cities.[12] Contrary to recent fashionable attitudes that man's work is inherently ugly and inferior, the townframe approach can complement the earth. Lhasa (Figure 2–30) and Mediterranean hill towns are archetypical images of complementary additions to landscapes.

Figure 2–30
View of Potala, the former residence of Dalai Lama in Lhasa, Tibet. Note: This megasize complex was begun in 1645, and the landscape is inconceivable without it.

SOCIAL AND PSYCHOLOGICAL IMPLICATIONS

The real influx of the problem will be felt in the already overtaxed cities, particularly in the Third World countries. Since time immemorial the city has embodied man's aspirations. Notwithstanding periodic returns to the simpler life on the land, the city has held out the promise of advancement and betterment. Man is a social being, and the human interactions and the social fermentation in the cites has been the prime moving force in the history of civilization. It is imperative that new building forms be found to further man's relationship with man.

The townframe is a stage where man can externalize his existence. In a context increasingly lacking in individual and community decision making, it is a building form receptive to such participation. Or, man can retreat to his home to restore his depleted energy by escaping the forced impersonal interaction of modern urban life. Subjected to mass housing, people have lost control over their physical environment. The townframe should permit us to be as open or as closed to our neighbors as we find desirable. Aldo van Eyck has said it very well:

Planning on whatever scale level should provide a framework

—to set the stage as it were—for the twin phenomenon of the individual and the collective without resorting to arbitrary accentuation of either one at the expense of the other . . . . [13]

According to James Burns, the social and psychological implications of megastructures holds the greatest promise to man:

Now we must find processes to create these new environments in ways that will enhance human life, gratify its energies, and contribute to interpersonal urban creativity. [14]

The social and psychological aspects of megastructures cannot be divorced from political and economic considerations. We would, however, be presumptuous to assume that the townframe is an instrument for restructuring society and that by building what amounts to an artificial landscape (this will be explored more in the next section), we can eliminate social and economic inequities. In this respect the idea of townframes is neutral. We can design a matrix that promotes individual incentive or furthers the collective, but we can not redistribute wealth through design.

The capitalist system with its private land ownership and accompanying land speculation is suspicious of planning that may in any way curtail exploitation. But townframes can be built by private capital perhaps more easily and with less bureaucracy than by government agencies. Coop City in New York, Reston, Virginia and Columbia, Maryland are examples of large-scale private developments in the United States. The capitalist system has recently suffered the most in the area of small-scale enterprises, and the phased approach to building could give it a shot in the arm. Lack of small parcels of land commensurate with available capital and methods of operation has affected the modest-size developer and individual owner-builder more than big developers.

The key aspect of capitalism has been its promise, whether real or illusory, of betterment of the human lot through individual initiative, success, and incentive. Social and economic mobility towards a "place in the sun" and "a piece of the action" has been at the expense of someone else. Unfortunately, this competitive force and greed have motivated most societies, and such attitudes cannot be changed through wishful thinking, indoctrination, or propaganda.

Individual incentive has been denied to peoples under communist regimes. Only their elite ruling class enjoys some upward mobility. The Soviet Union and its satellites are concerned not with the welfare of the individual but rather with control and regimentation in the interest of the state. A framework that promotes individual choice and may contribute to emergence of alternative modes of living is threatening to the vested interests of oppressive systems. China has shown much greater concern for its masses, and certainly environmental planning on a national scale has replaced wanton exploitation of the earth's resources. Conceivably, in China a framework could be designed that would foster community decisionmaking and would be tolerated, provided it does not threaten the system as a whole.

Attempts to educate the capitalist society to the need for planning and design are too feeble. The media tend to cater to the tastes and preferences of the lowest common denominator. Special interest groups and corporate lobbies scare the public with "creeping socialism." Massive building commitments do present a risk, and fear of ultimate subjugation is ever present. It is hard to imagine, however, more oppressive living accommodations than the private or public mass housing of capitalist and communist countries.

More immediate obstacles and sources of frustration for any well-intentioned proposal are the barriers erected by the modern capitalist state. Zoning, codes, labor union disputes and lobbying, jurisdiction between countless municipal departments, fear of accountability on the part of public officials, and so forth constitute the most formidable opposition to the best of intentions. "Revolutionary" building endeavors are viewed as a risk by members of the municipal–state–federal establishment. As a consequence, currently only public authorities with sufficient power to cut through bureaucracies can implement omnistructures.

The authority must gather the support of the community, yet generate a plan that transcends the immediate and popular. The design of the framework must be based on timeless criteria. Individual participation through infil is written into the act due to the very nature of townframes. The problem lies at the other end of the scale, as stated by Otto Piene:

. . . a typically American psychosis: a sense of guilt about planning an environment for many, of undemocratic treason in seeking the betterment of everybody's environment . . . . The feeling of guilt about planning for others has to be replaced by the pride of being an expert contributing things and ideas that others cannot contribute. [15]

In the past complex and extensive built environments have been brought about through the need for defense, preference for social and religious exclusiveness, convergence of related functions or environmental isolation. Medieval castles and monasteries with a considerable measure of self-sufficiency were early forms of omnistructures. Large transportation nodes have generated shopping centers, and hotel and exhibition complexes have latched themselves on to such interchanges. Ocean liners have been cited as models for omnibuildings. Future, orbiting space stations and moon or other planetary colonies most certainly will be to a considerable degree self-sustaining omnistructures. The question of "habitability" [16] will have to be a primary consideration if people are to live in these extreme environments.

Habitability, however, is equally crucial in earthly omnistructures, and townframes and must be expanded to include all design criteria essential to humane existence. The purpose of this study is not to catalog all the qualities of the environment necessary for urban life. This awareness is now beginning to emerge in man-environment studies, and many traditional settlements have had a good measure of these qualities.

Human contact, need for privacy, complexity, play areas for children of various ages, sense of participation for the old, richness in experience, and awareness of the rhythm of life are but a few of the necessities and qualities that should be easier to achieve within a townframe. Opportunities for their occurrence, however, cannot be left to chance: Many of these features must be designed in the framework. This aspect of the macrostructure is one that cannot be overly emphasized. Comparisons can be made with the repetitive anonymous gridiron street layouts and the life that they sustain versus the public paths, streets, plazas, arcades, ramps, bridges, and stairs of Italian towns, for example, with their inherent qualities. These and similar places in other cultures provide timeless models that have few modern counterparts.

Developing a community takes time. In a world that is increasingly transient, man is in search of a place where he can grow roots. If he is forced to remain mobile, he looks for markers of times past: familiar forms and materials, signs of permanence, expressions that conjure associations and personal experience, exceptional craftsmanship, and other manifestations of human touch. The townframe approach to building, particularly if it is phased or integrated with the existing urban fabric, provides myriad possibilities for a human environment. Older buildings and neighborhoods can be incorporated with new connections or as free standing elements. Natural and cultural landscapes likewise can contribute to the uniqueness of each townframe. The anonymous framework itself can communicate a sense of permanence and security in a physically and socially changing world.

There are then considerable prospects that townframes and omnistructures through their inherent comprehensiveness, continuity, and possible transformations may contain the seeds of a very exciting and more humane environment unachievable by fragmented individual buildings. We know where the present course is taking us. The time has come to put the townframe concept to the test.

MEGAFORM VERSUS GROUP FORM

A townframe is a manmade landscape. It may end up as megaform, or what Maki calls group form.[17] A megaform is a concise linear, planar, or spatial framework—that is, a megabuilding (Figure 2–31). Group form in building is an aggregation or clustered mass of individual elements (Figure 2–32). It results from incremental assembly of buildings that may or may not recognize their interdependence and relationship to site. Japanese and Dogon villages and Greek hill towns are commonly recognized examples of group form.

Megascale frameworks do not necessarily need to end up as megaforms. They have the potential to grow randomly and incrementally and to accommodate internal elements analogous to the Mediterranian dwelling environments. Such a structure then would be representative of a hierarchic group form: an aggregation of individual building elements within larger-scale meandering framework clusters (Figure 2–33).

Hitherto, most megaform proposals have ended up as monoliths because such structures are more easily conceived. They are, by and large, extensions of our existing buildings and engineering works. Maki claims that the elements in the megaform are determined by the skeleton but that group form is evolved by the people.[18] Such has been the case until now because the elements—the infil—were also determined

and arranged by the designers of the megaform—the macrostructure—who have been too eager to put the framework to maximum use.

Just as the implied or actual links in group form are the ordering principles in indigenous settlements, the framework will definitely guide growth and affect the nature of the elements. A rectilinear macrostructure is more likely to further right angle geometries within; a more complex framework will exert demands on the user and the designer of infil systems. The user has to confront his space-lot volume, ponder its implications, and decide how to best take advantage of his site, location, and space. Designing and building in the complex framework is harder but also much more rewarding and educating. The amount of infil will also emerge over time, thus further approximating evolution of group form.

Current megaform proposals are testimonials to our poor imagination. Stacked full of units with only token variations, they represent a cosmetic illusion of choice and variety rather than the preference of the inhabitants. Given an opportunity to order their own immediate environment, people in time will evolve contemporary indigenous architecture with complexities reflecting the richness or for that matter the monotony of their lives. Thus, the group form within a skeleton is contingent on attitudes and policies conducive to user-determined housing.

SCALE AND FORM

The question of scale in architecture remains unresolved and a source of considerable emotional confrontation. Everyone professes expertise in the subject, but, curiously enough, studies in scale are conspicuously lacking.

The sixties and seventies can not be described as a heroic period in architecture. While hopelessness and absence of identifiable models characterize man's

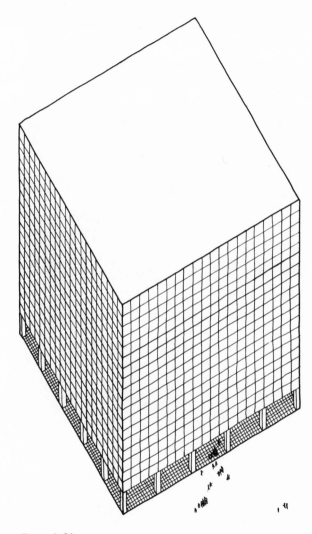

Figure 2-31
An abstracted megaform. Note: A megaform is a massive volume—that is, a megabuilding of a superhuman scale. Place Bonaventure (Figure 2–15) is a built megaform.

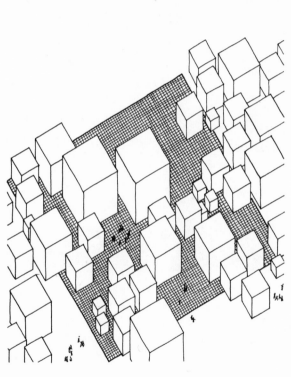

Figure 2-32
An abstracted group form. Note: Group form results from clustering of individual elements. Mediterranean hill towns are group forms.

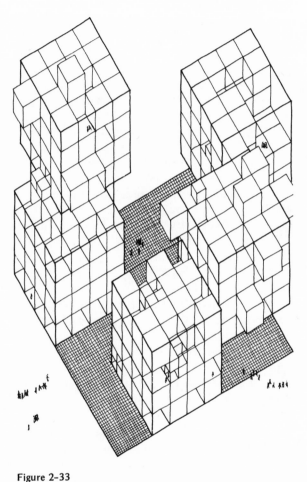

Figure 2-33
An abstracted hierarchic group form. Note: This form is an aggregation of individual building elements within a larger-scale group form. A system within a system within a system can be the principle of the order of a hierarchic group form. There are no readily identifiable built hierarchic group forms.

lack of confidence in himself and his future, this is not necessarily an entirely unwelcome state. Deflation of the feeling of omnipotence may well be essential to our survival. Yet this very period has witnessed man's journey to the moon and his first timid steps beyond the home planet.

Throughout history the artist has been at the forefront of society. Today he has dared to explore the impact of art on a scale hitherto mostly confined to engineering works. Earthforms, Christo's curtains stretching across landscapes, pneumatic arches swaying over ice, and beams of light dissecting the night skies are but some of the environmental art forms (Figure 2–34). These have contributed to awareness of forces and phenomena seldom experienced.

Attitudes in architecture, however, are quite different. The surest way to a pro-human stance is to be critical of any large building or structure per se. This stand immediately labels the proclaimer a humanitarian, for ". . . human scale is somewhat akin to motherhood—it is supposed to be never changing, always desirable, and beyond questioning."[19] Yet the Gothic cathedrals and freeway interchanges were not built by and for giants. They are manifestations of man's spiritual and physical needs and are products of humanity as much as a New England farmhouse or for that matter one eighteenth of an inch square microcircuit.

Difficulties obviously are caused by terminology. For milennia, "human scale" has meant "bodily scale." The human body has been the measure of all things. Human height, arm spread, sight line, and audio and walking range have shaped the surroundings. Brick size was determined by the hand; the shovel was a modest extension of the palm. As the horse altered the range and speed of travel, the machine and the discovery of electricity extended human capacity and experience beyond all conceivable limits. Part of the collective consciousness, the boundless experiential realm is irreversible short of total discontinuity in

Figure 2–34
"Sculpture in Suspension" by Jan Zach (1968) in Eugene, Oregon. Note: This environmental sculpture was made of Rockwell stainless steel with a silvery-frosted surface and suspended by steel cables and nylon ropes from four 40' wooden poles in an area 100' by 60'. The three bell-like shapes are about 25' wide and 16' high and measure about 80' in length. In addition to the interesting play of light upon the forms, the surfaces have unusual acoustic properties that contribute to a fresh environmental experience. (Photograph courtesy of Jan Zach, University of Oregon.)

human development. Thus, as pointed out by Jan Rowan, "human scale" understood in its narrowest bodily terms is animal scale.[20]

The history of mankind is an endless quest to rise above our animal past. Despite the resulting problems, our technological extensions have been instrumental in this development. Evolution of contemporary human scale is impossible without recognition of these extensions.

Considered in its narrower perceptual-psychological way, scale in architecture is used to describe the relationship between the size of a building or an element of it to man. Modern buildings through their anonymous wrappings have undermined this relationship. No longer can we tell the thickness of floors, the location and existence of mechanical equipment on roof or on other levels, the presence of structure, the nature of the skin, or even the number of floors. Enclosed in mirror glass or covered with a uniform grid, buildings lack all scale-giving clues. Small wonder that we can only react to their size, and even that is obscured.

The architect has not learned from nature that change in size is accompanied by change in form. This lack of understanding may be due to the fact that we have seldom been forced to consider optimum structural and environmental conditions. Any absurdity can be built, and fashion most often dictates the shape of the building.

A small organism, such as a worm, can take on all of its needed oxygen through its smooth skin. A tenfold increase in dimension will increase its weight one thousand times and surface area one hundred times, provided its shape is unaltered. The worm will not be able to take on ten times more oxygen without developing compensating organs, such as gills or lungs. "The higher animals are not larger than the lower because they are more complicated. They are more complicated because they are larger."[21] There are, of course, buildings that force us to similar considerations of form. Standard elevators in multistory buildings could conceivably occupy the majority of floor area if they stopped at each floor. Why we need to build that high is, of course, another question, but zoning the elevators into express and locals, plus introduction of sky-lobby transfer floors has made using such buildings possible. The structure of tall buildings, likewise, has its dimensional realm. Whether rigid frame, frame-shear truss, belt truss, framed, trussed and bundled tubes, each has its limits.[22] By these standards, even with atomic powered elevators, F. L. Wright's Mile High Illinois is but a "King Kong"

among buildings—that is, a physical impossibility in its conceived form.

The force of gravity and limitations in mechanical systems, however, have only affected the expression of buildings where the boundaries of the possible have been challenged. Even these physical systems are seldom visible and understandable to a layman in as straightforward a manner as the annual growth rings in a tree. Most of the other physical forces are not even recognized. The building is covered with an anonymous envelope identical on all sides and devoid of any scale-giving elements on outside as well as inside. Columns, mullions, moldings, gaskets, reveals, and so forth, if present at all, are not different on a large building than on a more modestly sized structure. There are only more of them. The gap between the human body and the size of the building becomes so large that any assessment of the extent of the structure is difficult.

Increasing the size of building details and elements is seldom possible. Relative scale, as in St. Peter's does not relate to the human body without the presence of man. Most modern building materials are limited in size, but devoid of scale-giving clues: textures, grain, and imperfections in material. Even the fabrication markings are carefully erased.

Scale in architecture is hierarchic. This hierarchy results from two distinct modes of organization or the combination of the two. Aggregation of identical elements or progressive change in the nature of the elements are the two extreme modes. In building, an infinite assembly of basically identical elements is a physical impossibility. The concrete modules in Safdie's Habitat are made to look more or less the same to convey the potential of mass production, but they are significantly different from top to bottom. There is a progressive change in the amount of reinforcing within the concrete walls. Yet the trusting observer is tricked into believing that such building blocks can be stacked to these heights. This feat

would be possible only in a nongravity environment or with elements (soap bubbles) that are not appreciably affected by gravity.

Physical forces rather than machine production determine the economy in repetition in some dimensional realms. Bolts can be of the same size, but the thickness of glass may have to increase or the size decrease towards the top of a high-rise building. And then again one may need to switch to larger bolts or closer spacing as well. Using the same piece throughout has been so easy that we have not explored the scale-giving potential of construction components.

The fundamental truth in nature that each thing is restricted to a dimensional latitude applies to the built environment as well as to mosquitoes, birds, and airplanes.

Nucleons bind together to make nuclei of relatively fixed size, electrons join nuclei to make atoms of a well-defined magnitude, atoms unite to form molecules, molecules combine to make cells, and cells make organisms. You never find a nucleus, an atom, a molecule or a cell as big as a man. Each form has its own dimensional realm, its upper and lower bounds. But each form combines and works together with others like itself to make larger structures and organizations.[23]

The greatest opportunity for giving scale to larger buildings and megascale structures lies in the realm of human requirements. The social and psychological needs of people are conspicuously absent from such projects. Major and minor public "centers of life," internal pedestrian streets, sky lobbies, roof gardens, balconies, and other connections with the environment, bridges to other structures, contact between the floors and visibility-of-movement systems are but some of the most obvious scale-giving features of megascale building endeavors. The all too rare incorporation of some of these facilities has met with astounding success. John Portman's interior of the Hyatt Regency Hotel in San Francisco, the nineteenth-century interiors typified by the Bradbury building in

Los Angeles, and the less widely known "Man the Producer" pavilion of Expo '67 (Figures 2-10, 2-11, and 2-35) give some indication of the possible. The human dimension, however, as pointed out by James Fitch,[24] is absent in the high-rise buildings that, curiously, have received little architectural development since Louis Sullivan. The suprascale problems and possibilities resulting from close-packing of towers have been ignored. Scale-giving and humanizing flying streets with cafes, playgrounds, theatres, bars, parks, kiosks, and so forth do not exist.

If change in size is accompanied by change in form, then increase in scale, likewise, must reflect change in meaning. Form is the result of internal needs as well as the result of forces that act upon it or a record of past imprints. It reflects processes that brought it about and communicates its role in the physical realm. Form has meaning. Consequently, simple enlargement of a thing without a corresponding change in form transforms the meaning of the object or its context. The well-publicised Claes Oldenburg's giant toilet float in the Thames achieves precisely that. There is a considerable range in expression of most modest size buildings. Although physically increasing the size of these buildings may at times be possible, such increase is at the expense of environmental and human considerations. Equally demanding criteria in the design of megascale structures inevitably will result in forms uniquely associated with such environments. Inclusion of the human act will also return bodily scale to the technological dimensions.

Figure 2-35
Interior opening over a canal in "Man the Producer" theme pavilion of Expo '67 in Montreal by Affleck, Desbarats, Dimakopoulos, Lebensold, and Sise, Architects. Note: Designed to absorb queues and to permit alternative circulation routes with a multitude of decks, sloping walls and views, the organic-seeming space structure is a stage for people. As space for space's sake, it transcends its functional purpose. (Photograph by Michael Schellenbarger, University of Oregon.)

3

The Nature of Space-Lot Frameworks

Basic studies of space-lot frameworks do not exist at this time. There certainly is a wealth of information on housing and a number of proposals of similar housing structures. In our eagerness to visualize the results, we are likely to bypass basic "obvious" concepts. Realistic and detailed development of architectural proposals inevitably results in loss of universality. A particular project may not disclose the basic principles, differences, and possible alternatives common to space-lot frameworks. A more general study is needed for this purpose.

The model framework described in Chapter 5 must be preceded by more abstract comparisons between prevailing building types and the nature of space-lot frameworks. Through a juxtaposition with the familiar and common it is hoped that the differences will become much more clear and the reasoning behind the development of such frameworks apparent. Consequently, the design of the model framework is one application of the general prototype and next to actual construction a concretization of the abstract.

To abstract is to reduce something to its essentials or to uncover the universal underlying principles. In the hands of the designer, these principles take on meaning. The same basic abstraction manifests itself in a thousand different ways. The particular needs, context, methods, and materials mold the abstract beyond recognition, thereby rendering it unique. Consequently, this chapter attempts to identify the nature of space-lot frameworks by abstracting them to their essential components and relationships. Emphasis is placed on the typical rather than the unique, special, or accidental. Only the most significant aspects are presented here.

The chapter consists primarily of a pictorial sequence with brief text comments rather than a detailed discussion of such frameworks. Graphic means are more direct and useful for establishing basic requirements and illustrating differences. User-adapted space-lot frameworks are contrasted with typical, ordinary housing types for easier comparison.

Identification of all the characteristics, forms, and processes instrumental in generation and transformation of three-dimensional frameworks is beyond the capacity of this book. In the absence of built examples, a more exhaustive study may well be premature and could become an academic exercise at this time.

SPACE LOTS VERSUS AVAILABLE HOUSING

Apartment Buildings

Apartment buildings evolved because mankind lacked technology, resources, and a will to develop socially–psychologically–environmentally supportive high-density dwellings. Such compartmentalization (Figure 3-1) was accepted as an inevitable consequence of urban life. Apartment buildings:

result in closely packed cells that preclude additions and change;
rarely permit rearrangement of rooms;
discourage personalization of one's dwelling;
divorce man from the building process;
remove man from contact with society and nature;
result in generalized accommodations or require excessive initial and continuous design service.

Many apartment buildings, such as the one on Nuns Island in Montreal (Figure 3-2) may well be works of art or precious objects, but the role of the individual has been confined to passive containment. Much has been said about the architect's control of drapes and the packaging of such containers. The boldness of the form of the Montreal building is undeniable, but the aesthetic of change and the degree of control presents a design challenge that has yet to be explored.

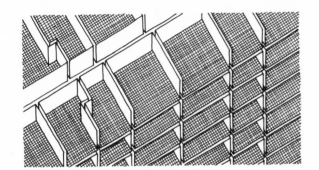

Figure 3-1
Apartment building compartmentalization.

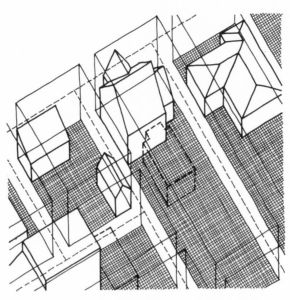

Figure 3-3
Individual houses as enclosures within a legal spatial envelope.

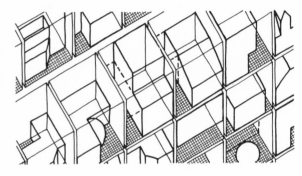

Figure 3-5
High-density space lots.

Figure 3-2
Apartment building on Nuns Island in Montreal by Mies van der Rohe.

Figure 3-4
A house in Eugene, Oregon.

Individual Houses

Individual houses constitute the most ideal dwellings. In many parts of an increasingly urbanized world, the house no longer is an attainable building. Resulting destruction of valuable land and overextended lines of communication make the individual house unacceptable as an urban structure (Figure 3–3). Individual houses:

allow for personalization and choice in one's dwelling;

permit additions within the setbacks and height restrictions;

provide children with play areas;

bring inhabitants in contact with soil and vegetation and permit gardening;

give the inhabitants the satisfaction of ownership and identity;

provide more space and permit acquisition of recreational equipment and vehicles;

permit the owner to share in the building process;

give the inhabitants the feeling that they can do as they please.

The house shown in Figure 3–4 was moved to its present location and has been owned by several families. The previous owners added on, revised the interior, and did some landscaping. Once again it is undergoing major repairs and changes in the interior and in landscaping. It can be maintained or allowed to deteriorate. Such older homes are much in demand; yet the ideal home is bound to become extinct. Since the summer of 1975 the average American family can no longer afford to purchase a house.

High-Density Space Lots

High-density space lots (Figure 3–5) would integrate the individual houses in residential frameworks.

Such frameworks can include as many of the amenities of a house or, for that matter, rental units as feasible. High density space lots:

can establish boundaries for self-expression and choice in urban housing;

can return the control of man's immediate environment to the users;

can permit additions, change, and landscaping within each space lot;

can separate the design and construction of the space-lot infil from the framework and all access and support systems;

can increase the life span of the built environment;

can be less destructive of natural resources than other housing types;

can contribute to the social and psychological well-being of the inhabitants.

Figure 3–6 depicts the simulated infil of space lots (see also Figure 5–34). Houses, apartments, and gardens can be built within urban frameworks that provide access and services. Volumes analogous to setbacks in residential neighborhoods can provide the prospective owner of a space lot with similar freedom of choice.

Figure 3–6
Simulated infil of space lots. (Gary Day, University of Oregon, 1974.)

SPATIAL NEEDS

There are no absolute requirements for the amount and nature of occupiable space. Figure 3–7 depicts the proportions of closely packed space lots and the relationship to inner pedestrian street and outside. The pros and cons of the lettered space lots shown in the figure are discussed below. All of the space lots are of approximately equal size volumes.

Figure 3–7
Proportions of closely packed space lots and relationship to inner pedestrian street and outside.

Space Lot A. *Pros:* Maximum exposure to light and air

Closest possible proximity to the ground floor

Cons: Extended circulation within the lot

Limited choice in room size, shape, and arrangement

Extensive outside surface area

Increased length of the inner street and horizontal utilities

Space Lot B. *Pros:* Good exposure to light and air if service spaces are arranged along the pedestrian street

Closest possible proximity to the ground floor

Cons: Rather limited choice in room shape and arrangement

Somewhat long inner street front and long horizontal utilities

Space Lot C. *Pros:* Reasonable choice in room size and arrangement within the limitations of a single story

Closest possible proximity to the ground floor

Cons: Some rooms must face and get light and air from the inner street

Space Lot D. *Pros:* Maximum exposure to light and air

Choice in height of rooms

Vertical zoning of activities

Cons: Increased height of the support structure

Increased distance to ground for all but the lowest lot

Space Lot E. *Pros:* Maximum exposure to light and air

Choice in height of rooms

Cons: Limited area per floor

Unavoidable, excessive stair climbing

Further increase in height of support structure resulting also in excessive elevator runs and increased length of vertical utilities

Space Lot F. *Pros:* Compact interior circulation

Choice in room size, shape, and arrangement

Optimum length of pedestrian street and depth of support structure

Space Lot G. *Cons:* Volume used by stairs resulting in extreme stair climbing and unusable spaces

Space Lot H. *Pros:* Limited length of the inner pedestrian street and horizontal utilities

Choice in height of rooms

Cons: Limited area per floor

Unavoidable, excessive stair climbing

High support structure and long vertical utilities

Increased distance to ground for all but the lowest lots

Space Lot I. *Pros:* Limited length of the pedestrian street and horizontal utilities

Choice in height of rooms

Vertical zoning of activities

Cons: Some rooms must face and get light and air from the inner pedestrian street

Space Lot J. *Pros:* Reasonable choice in room size and arrangement within the limitations of a single story

Closest possible proximity to the ground floor

Cons: Some rooms must face and get light and air from the pedestrian street

Space Lot K. *Pros:* Short pedestrian streets and horizontal utility runs

Closest possible proximity to the ground floor

Cons: Rooms must face inner street for light and air

Limited choice in room shape and arrangement

Space Lot L. *Pros:* Minimum length of inner pedestrian streets and horizontal utilities

Closest possible proximity to the ground floor

Cons: Interior rooms without light and air

Extended circulation within the lot

Limited choice in room size, shape, and arrangement

Minimum spatial needs. Perhaps one should be able to pitch a tent within the volume of a space lot as on any other site (Figure 3-8). Spatial needs and financial means vary greatly, and Figure 3-9 depicts a typical example of a home that satisfies minimum size needs.

Normal spatial needs. Average family needs may increase over years and spatial requirements change. Room must be allowed for such changes, and the space lot must include some outside area (Figure 3-10). Reasonable expansion of an average size dwelling is then the determining factor of dominant space-lot sizes. Figure 3-11 depicts a home that satisfies normal spatial needs.

Maximum spatial needs. Determining extensive space requirements (Figure 3-12) is difficult. The wealthy can acquire as much additional space as necessary. Extended families may want to move into larger space-lot volumes. The poor are most crammed because several families may share the dwelling. Paradoxically, their spatial needs may also be greater due to various home shops and other attempts at economic survival. Figure 3-13 depicts a home that can provide for maximum spatial needs.

Figure 3-8
Minimum space-lot volume.

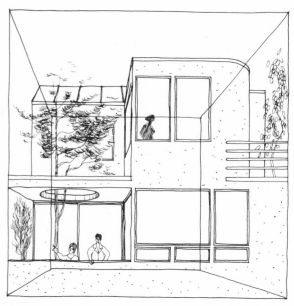

Figure 3-10
Normal spatial needs.

Figure 3-9
A minimum-sized house on an average size lot in Manhattan, Kansas.

Figure 3-11
A normal-sized house on an average size lot in Manhattan, Kansas.

Figure 3-12
Extensive spatial needs.

Figure 3-13
A large house on an average size lot in Manhattan, Kansas.

SPATIAL GEOMETRY

Rectilinear spatial geometry. Rectilinear spaces are easiest to use (Figure 3-14), but their stability is dependent on rigid connections and material mass. Vertical stacking of such bending-resistant structures results in bulky members. Rectilinear megascale frameworks inevitably end up very heavy and consequently are expensive to build. Necessary continuity and rigid connections frustrate changes and renewal. Although spatially advantageous, these structures are the least efficient.

Triangular spatial geometry. Triangular spaces are difficult to use (Figure 3-15), particularly if the spatial modules are relatively small. Loss of space due to the sloping angles decreases with increase in size of such geometry. Some of this loss is offset by the minimum size of members. Triangulated geometries result in the most efficient and versatile structures, and they are well suited to space-lot frameworks. Although trusses have been around for a long time, the architectural potential of triangulated geometry has not been sufficiently explored.

Curved spatial geometry. Curved spaces, such as domes, are fairly easy to use provided they do not need to be subdivided (Figure 3-16). Spherical surfaces are the most efficient enclosures of volumes. Contemporary curved structure systems, however, do not lend themselves to stacking; curved spatial geometry is not suited as a primary structure system of space-lot frameworks.

Space lots such as those shown in Figure 3-17 do not need to be completely filled in from the start. An initial minimal dwelling can be located anywhere within the available volume (top sequence in the figure). Additions, in turn, can be located anywhere in relation to the existing dwelling (middle sequence). Incremental additions are possible until the volume is filled.

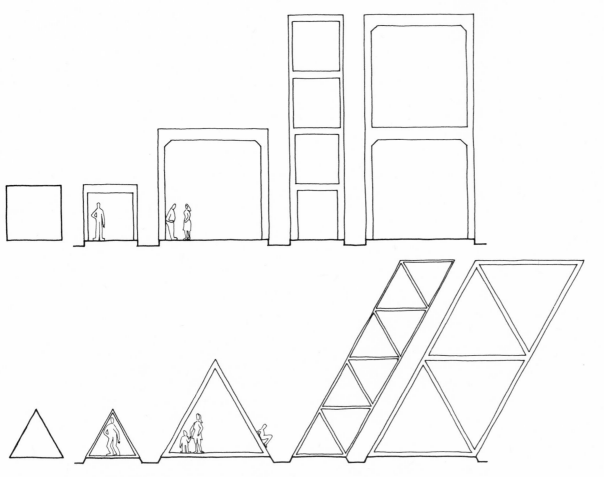

Figure 3-14
Rectilinear spatial geometry, structure, and stacking.

Figure 3-15
Triangular spatial geometry, structure, and stacking.

Figure 3-16
Curved spatial geometry and structure.

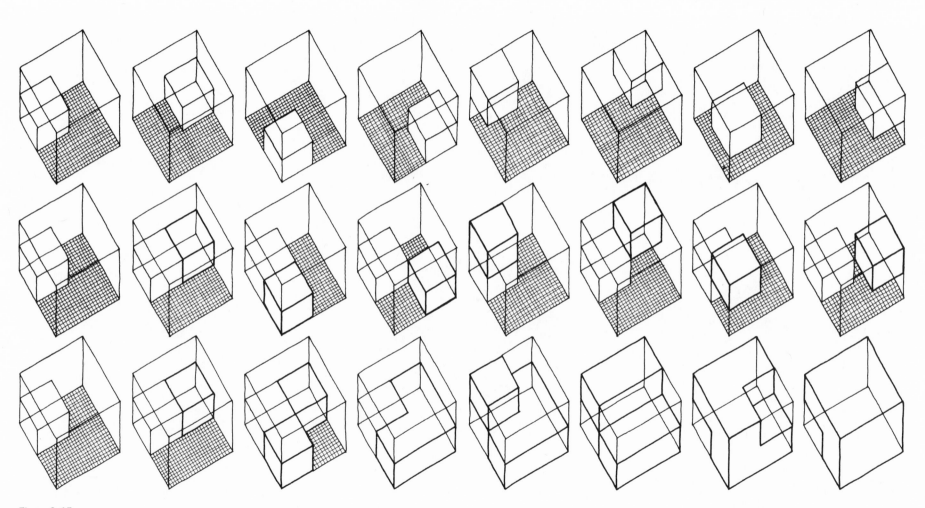

Figure 3-17
Variability in amount and location of enclosed space within a space lot.

HOUSING TYPE ADAPTABILITY TO SPACE-LOT FRAMEWORKS

Inevitably space-lot frameworks will have unique and recognizable forms distinct from current housing. The model framework described in Chapter 5 is one attempt at such a development. Transition, however, is likely to come from prevailing housing types. First cars were carriages with the engines as substitute horses. Thus a critique of the adaptability of existing housing types to space-lot frameworks should precede a search for forms unique to such frameworks.

Individual, detached dwellings, (Figure 3-18) constitute the optimum form for owner-built or -controlled housing. As stated earlier, a house is an unattainable form of shelter in areas of an urbanizing world and a building type that contributes to the urban sprawl.

Row houses (Figure 3-19) are equally conducive to the user-completed building process. Fire walls can provide the structure for subsequent infil and define the limits of building and possession. Beams or trusses or attachments for such structural members, utility cores, and other elements or clues can further aid the owner or subsequent designer in the completion of the dwelling.

Walk-up–height cluster housing types (Figure 3-20) could be built as frameworks for user-controlled environments. These are likely to require greater ingenuity on the part of the framework designer due to potential conflicts. The limited height permits relatively easy construction of the infil systems and delivery of materials. Cluster type frameworks would require a

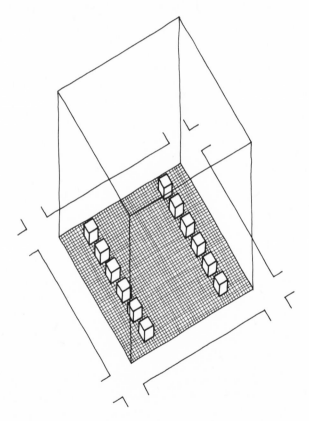

Figure 3-18
Individual, detached dwellings.

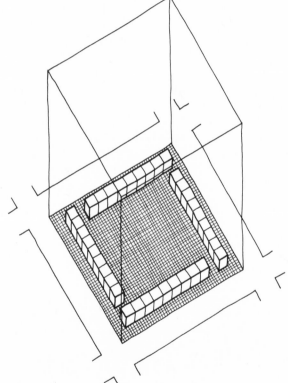

Figure 3-19
Row houses.

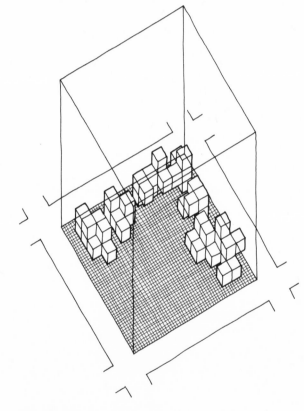

Figure 3-20
Walk-up–height cluster housing.

number of safeguards, such as visual barriers and pre-scribed materials to guarantee some degree of privacy and to minimize offensive conditions.

Walk-up-height linear housing forms (Figure 3-21) can be easily adapted to frameworks for user-controlled dwellings. These can take on a variety of configurations depending on their circulation, structural system, terrain and other conditions (see Figures 4-3, 5-1, and 5-2). Construction materials can be lifted into place by fork-lift trucks or small cranes with minimal disruption of the grounds.

High-rise apartment towers (Figure 3-22), regardless of their social and psychological impact, are ill suited to user-controlled space-lot frameworks. Space necessary for internal vertical and horizontal movement of materials would considerably increase the size of the core and thus render such frameworks uneconomical. External lifting of material or ready-built modules requires a built-in crane throughout the duration of the framework. High-rise towers came about through the invention of the steel frame and the elevator rather than optimum living conditions.

High-rise apartment slabs (Figure 3-23) similar to towers are not ideal forms for user-controlled space-lot frameworks due to the limited use of a service elevator and the lack of continuity of internal horizontal access ways. Once again, the narrow corridors would have to increase considerably in width. Jamming space lots into building forms that are often derived from aesthetic considerations would not constitute an acceptable design procedure.

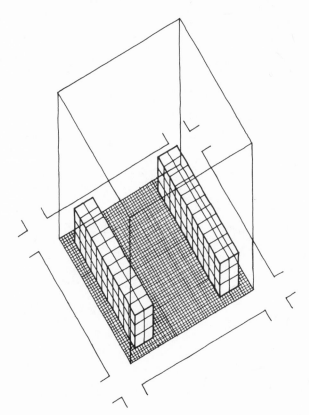

Figure 3-21
Walk-up-height linear housing.

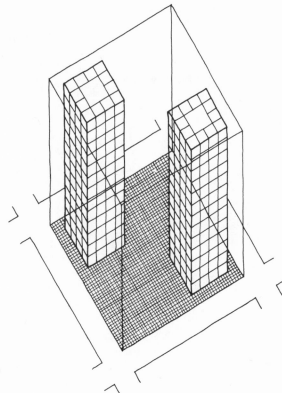

Figure 3-22
High-rise apartment towers.

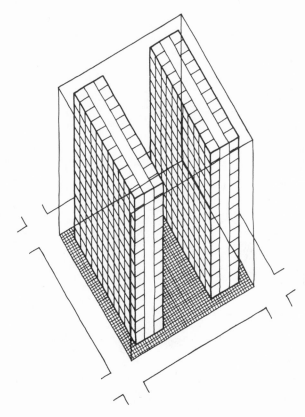

Figure 3-23
High-rise apartment slabs.

Linear, terraced frameworks (Figure 3-24) provide suitable sites for user-controlled housing due to easy horizontal access and possible continuity over city blocks. These structures may form part of a hillside or connect directly to land in other ways, thereby eliminating the need for service elevators.

Large, Habitat-like terraced clusters (Figure 3-25) could also provide the context for user-controlled space lots. Access, however, could be more problematic. As in the walk-up height clusters, these would require considerable controls to preclude conflicts in use. A system of walls could not only minimize interference but also give clues to the users on the more advantageous utilization of the volumes.

Continuous space-grid frameworks (Figure 3-26) begin to generate user-controlled townframes with sites for housing as well as commercial office and entertainment strips that are integrated into or spill out of the framework. Production of infil systems, building material recycling centers, and communal energy generating facilities needs an economic base that larger developments are more likely to provide.

There is considerable variety of forms and systems applicable to space-grid townframes.

Examples and Comparisons

High-rise, slab-type apartment buildings (Figure 3-27) with double-loaded corridors and token balconies are very common. Variations in plan, unit types, or the treatment of the facade do not basically change the prototype.

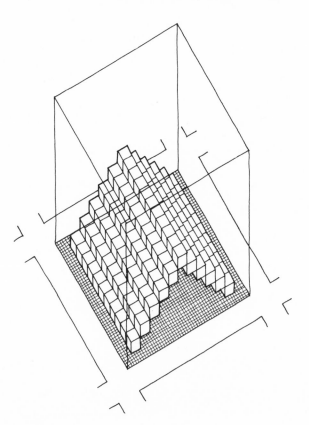

Figure 3-24
Linear, terraced framework.

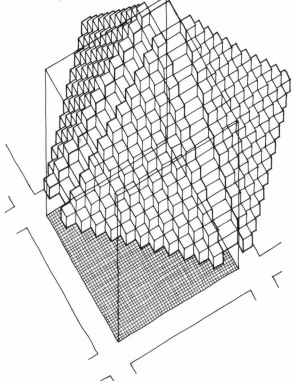

Figure 3-25
Terraced clusters.

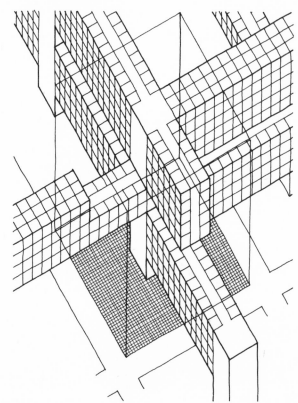

Figure 3-26
Continuous space-grid framework.

A comparative example of double-loaded space-lot framework is shown in Figure 3-28. Each space lot is two-and-a-half stories high and of the same size for easier comparison with high-rise housing. Consequently, these space-lots take up two and a half times the volume as the apartments shown in Figure 3-27. The additional space allows for growth and change within each lot, provides for outside garden areas, and assures a longer period of stay within the framework.

Figure 3-29 depicts a comparative example of a single-loaded space-lot framework with lots on the lower floor without a separation from the surrounding grounds. This terraced scheme integrates parking on one side and provides for a commercial and entertainment strip above the parking structure. Dwellings within the space lots can face each way because the pedestrian walkways are open to the air.

Figure 3-30 depicts the internal circulation system *only* of typical apartment buildings: a high-rise, slab-type building, a multistory apartment building, and a low-rise walk-up apartment building with an internal corridor. The floors below ground level are not shown to eliminate confusion. Most of these buildings provide no visual contact with the outside. The corridors are too narrow for delivery of building materials and there are no transition areas between the hallways and the apartments. Current research has pointed out the alienating social and pscyhological consequences of living in such high-rise buildings.

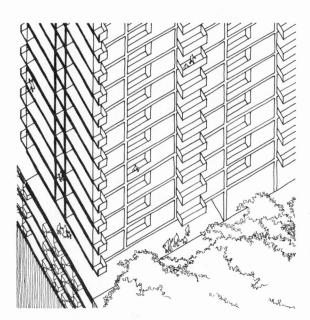

Figure 3-27
Common multistory apartment building.

Figure 3-28
Double-loaded space-lot framework.

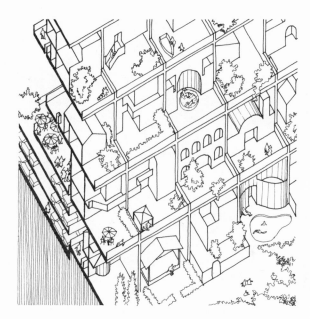

Figure 3-29
Single-loaded space-lot framework.

Figure 3-30
Internal circulation system of typical apartment buildings.

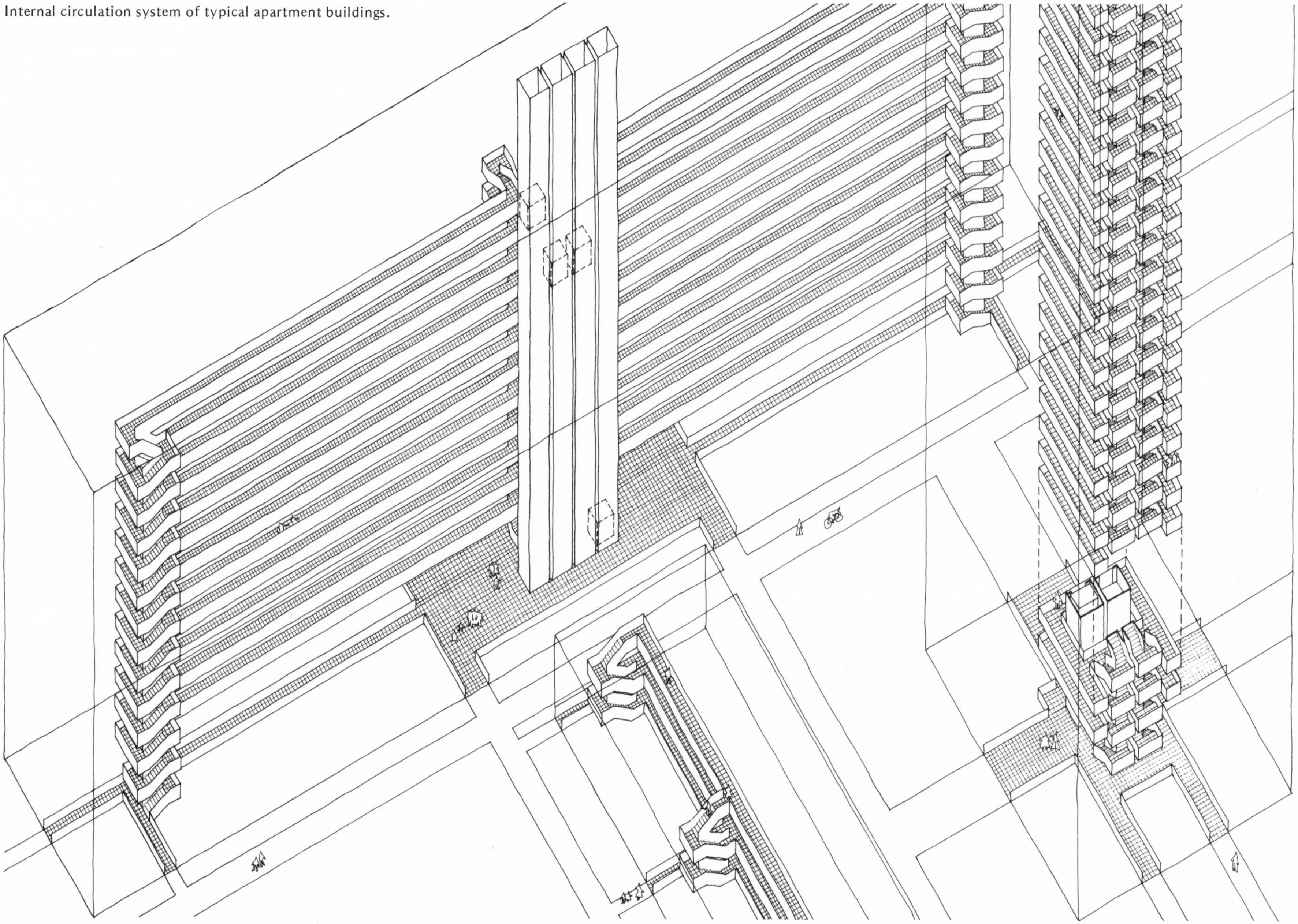

4

Some Criteria for High-Density Space Lots

The following criteria statements represent some of the key concerns that were instrumental in the design of the model framework developed in this study and are of importance to other high-density frameworks in applicable cultural and environmental contexts. They are far from complete.

This chapter is not an attempt to establish general planning and design criteria, such as Christopher Alexander's et al. pattern language[1] or William Kleinsasser's research in experiential criteria at the University of Oregon.[2] Although some parallels are inevitable, the aim is much more modest—that is, to identify only the most essential requirements of high-density user-adapted housing without which such frameworks could not exist. The reason is practical: Attempts at completeness could easily become a lifetime endeavor, and there is no need to duplicate other evolving applicable criteria.

The method used in this chapter consists of a statement of condition that must be satisfied, a brief statement of the reasons why, and a longer description of how the condition is satisfied, as well as accompanying notes and illustrations of applicable built examples or model studies.

Development of the model framework described in Chapter 5 constitutes the focus of this study. Photographs of the model framework and of a number of parallel student projects are used to illustrate the conditions essential to user-controlled housing.

Reliance primarily on model studies is unavoidable because there are no built space lots. An extensive search could perhaps produce some evidence of analogous examples among ordinary housing. Such examples, however, would have to be used with great care less the reader be led to believe that space lots are an existing reality. They certainly are not. One is continuously faced with pathetic attempts to accommodate basic existential needs in face of overwhelming odds. A bubble-like crib protruding beyond the bedroom wall of a high-rise apartment building is only a more extreme manifestation of pent-up frustrations.

Much more could be learned from indigenous architecture, particularly in parts of the world where people were forced for economic, environmental, or defense purposes to live closely together. Unfortunately, architects have been primarily interested in the forms of such settlements and not in the patterns of use and the forces that brought them about.

Future criteria statements will need to expand on and further clarify spatial and use requirements and focus on appropriate materials, requirements for gradual construction of the infil, safety, utility systems, and other aspects of space-lot frameworks.

CONDITION 1: USER CHOICE AND CHANGE

Change and choice must be possible within each space lot without dependence on and interference with the neighboring lots (Figures 4–1 and 4–2).

Why. This requirement is no different from that of a house on a private lot, and high-density housing should provide the same opportunities.

How. Each space lot is a separate cell that is able to undergo transformations independent of neighboring cells and the framework. Condition 1 is possible if the space-lots are not tightly packed together during the initial occupancy and there is sufficient volume for future expansion and the necessary building process (Figure 4–3). Establishment of limits defined by physical systems is tantamount to the very existence of user-controlled environments. Projecting beyond boundary lines into public space or towards the outside will create conflicting situations and interfere with someone else's view, light, sun, or privacy or will contribute to other initially unforeseeable problems and consequently decrease the livability of the entire framework.[3]

Figure 4–1
A simulated user completion of the model framework developed in this study, east elevation. Note: The structure (scale: $1/2'' = 1'\,0''$) was assembled by architectural design students and then became a context for their individual designs within a chosen space lot. The class tested three different phases of construction within each of their space lots and the photograph shows the more complete last phase. Several conflicting conditions were discovered in this exercise, and the privacy screens were introduced to eliminate some of them. (University of Oregon, 1974.)

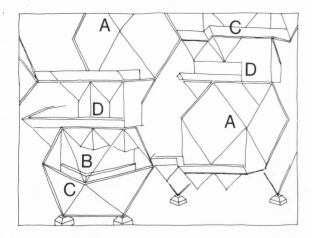

Figure 4-2
Space-lot sizes of the model framework (shown in Figure 4-1). Note: A is the maximum available space lot, or a complete cuboctahedral volume. B is the maximum space lot subdivided (the upper half of the cuboctahedra). C is the maximum space lot subdivided (the lower half of the cuboctahedra). D is the minimum available space lot, or the volume between the cuboctahedra.

Figure 4-3
A walk-up type of framework two levels high with two-story capacity within each space lot. Note: The open peripheral walkway separates the purchasable volumes and contains the mechanical systems. Each volume is then filled in to a different degree. In order to more realistically simulate the likely use of these space lots, the volume in the upper left was filled in by a student not experienced in design. (Bryan Croeni, University of Oregon, 1972.)

CONDITION 2: A LIVABLE ENVIRONMENT AT COMPLETION

Eventual "completion" of residences in the space lots to maximum limits must assure a livable environment.

Why. The framework may be most exciting and supportive when partially filled in, but saturation may result in oppressive conditions. The problem does not exist in apartment buildings and condominiums, as additions to apartments or other significant external changes are not possible.

How. The conditions of such saturation can be tested through simulated use (Figures 4-4 and 4-5) or by blocking in of maximum occupyable areas on each space lot. In fact, less desirable and uncontrollable conditions may at times occur when the residences are not "complete." Moderate use and amount of construction may underpopulate the framework, generate unanticipated wind patterns, or create some other unforeseen problems. This state may be somewhat analogous to unsold condominiums that consequently lack socially desirable density or the economic base for provision of services.

Figure 4-4
A view of the smallest empty space lot of the model framework from the southeast.

Figure 4–5

The smallest space lot of the model framework completely filled in. Note: The "owner" even uses the space between the 15' space trusses and quite imaginatively. The student found that the geometry of the design provided valuable clues to the use of the space. Initial attempts to get rid of some of the structure by several students were reversed as the design progressed. The design shown here originated among the space trusses above the main floor. The privacy screens shown in Figure 4–4 had not been designed and, in fact, the finished model did not yet exist. (Mohammad Maldjai, University of Oregon, 1974.)

CONDITION 3: USABLE AREAS
FOR EXPANSION

Minimum amount of enclosed area on a space lot should result in usable outdoor areas prior to expansion.

Why. Decks outside the space lot that are not initially built on or planned for may result in dark and oppressive areas that are difficult to use (Figure 4-6). Generally, concrete or other hard surfaces do not compare favorably with grass or even unmaintained weed- and dirt-covered areas.

How. There is no foolproof way to assure that the owner will locate his dwelling areas in the best place, anticipate his future needs, or even use his outside area. Available access, location of utilities, view, exposure, and other contextual factors, as well as prevailing cultural trends, provide powerful clues to building and use of available space. Decks and other surfaces that affect neighboring space lots must be built prior to occupation, but the decks must accept soil and the vertical planes of a variety of surface treatment.

Figure 4-6
Outdoor areas of a space lot. Note: Semi-basements, if not closed in, are difficult to use as leftover spaces for future expansion. This space would actually be much darker be- cause the terrace above was left off in the model. (B. Novitsky, University of Oregon, 1975.)

CONDITION 4: GARDEN AREAS

Space lots enclosed to maximum permissible limits must retain an outdoor garden area.

Why. Contact with nature is a basic human need particularly necessary in high-density environments (Figure 4-7). Exposure to nature's cycles brings man closer to the rhythm of life, perhaps even increases his awareness that his existence is part of this process. Proximity to vegetation and exterior play areas and the possibility of doing some gardening are just a few of the amenities usually denied apartment dwellers.

How. Initial provisions for and integration of such outdoor garden areas in the framework and limits on enclosable areas will assure their availability. Inclusion of "landscape modules" for growing small trees is possible through the use of the half-size space truss[4] (Figures 4-8, 4-9, and 4-10). The additional expenditure due to the large loads and necessary drainage systems is justifiable in view of the contribution small trees and shrubs make to a livable environment.[5] These artificial landscapes have the same potential for a unique environment as the small Japanese gardens; they can be aesthetically satisfying, and they provide daily contact with nature (Figures 4-11, 4-12, and 4-13).

Figure 4-7
A tree in San Francisco. Note: Certain trees can grow in the tightest places and provide daily enjoyment: shade, a place for birds, relief from the surrounding hard surfaces, and immeasurable aesthetic and sensory satisfaction.

Figure 4-8
A view of a large empty space lot of the model framework from the southwest.

Figure 4-9
The large space lot of the model framework filled in with a spatially exciting dwelling for an extended family. The "owners" have turned their outside area into a formal garden. (Gary Bail, University of Oregon, 1975.)

Figure 4-10
A garden area of the model framework. Note: A fence separates the more common entrance yard next to the inner pedestrian street from a private garden. Climbing plants cling and trail from the structure. The inhabitants can choose between growing grapes, ornamental plants, tomatoes, or cherries, or perhaps specializing in arranging rocks. (Gary Day, University of Oregon, 1974.)

Figure 4-11
A garden in Kyoto, Japan (Tanabe residence). Note: Japanese residential gardens provide intimate contact with changing seasons.

Figure 4-12
Arrangement of elements in a garden in Kyoto, Japan (Tanabe residence). Note: Masterfully arranged trees, shrubs, stones, and other elements accentuate perspective and alter the perception of space. The bamboo-clad wall behind the lantern was no more than twelve feet from the sliding glass and wood walls. Without the garden, the eight-mat room would have felt oppressively small.

Figure 4-13
A very small entrance garden to a Japanese restaurant in the Gion district of Kyoto, Japan.

CONDITION 5: ALLOWING FOR CHANGE OVER TIME

The framework must permit evolution of individual dwellings over a long period of time.

Why. Spatial needs of families change from year to year; yet their financial means do not initially permit ownership of large dwellings. Human existence is intimately related to the physical environment and the need to manipulate this environment is manifest in the possession of a home.

How. The framework can exist independent of the nature and amount of construction on the space lots. Likewise, available volume for building of dwellings on most space lots allows for future expansion and change. Figures 4–14 to 4–21 show gradual changes in a space-lot dwelling in a framework over a simulated fifteen-year period. The framework provided south-facing terraced volumes off pedestrian streets.) Thus a high-density residential structure can accommodate and reflect ongoing processes associated with living and the passage of time.

Figure 4–14
First floor of the initial dwelling in a framework designed by the student for a couple with three children ranging in age from four to ten. Note: The wife is an artist with a studio space at home (on the lower floor). A 73-year-old uncle who can not climb stairs also lives with the family and has a room that faces the triangular back garden. (Greg Stock, Kansas State University, 1976.)

Figure 4–15
Second floor of the initial dwelling. (Greg Stock, Kansas State University, 1976.)

Figure 4-16
The initial enclosed dwelling. (Greg Stock, Kansas State University, 1976.)

Figure 4-17
First floor of the dwelling in a framework ten years later. Note: Some changes have occurred in the family makeup and interests. The uncle has moved out, and the husband has started a small bicycle repair shop. The oldest child is now in college and comes home only on weekends. (Greg Stock, Kansas State University, 1976.)

Figure 4-18
Second floor of the dwelling ten years later. (Greg Stock, Kansas State University, 1976.)

Figure 4-19
The enclosed dwelling ten years later. (Greg Stock, Kansas State University, 1976.)

Figure 4-20
Second floor of the dwelling in a framework fifteen years later. Note: Part of the upstairs has been converted into a small apartment because the children have moved out. (Greg Stock, Kansas State University, 1976.)

Figure 4-21
The enclosed dwelling fifteen years later. (Greg Stock, Kansas State University, 1976.)

CONDITION 6: THE IMAGE OF PERMANENCE

The framework itself must reflect permanence and a sense of stability and continuity for the inhabitants.

Why. The framework's image of permanence and its integration into the landscape determine initial acceptance and occupation. Internal growth and development is unlikely to occur unless the inhabitants can become attached to their environment. Significant user construction, desire to remain in the framework, and pride in the property are unlikely to happen if the framework is threatened with disintegration.

How. The framework (Figure 4–22) can be designed to last hundreds of years with capacity for renewal and transformation without destruction. There is no reason why it could not last thousands of years, if initial plans and construction allow for the replacement of parts and systems when the need arises (Figure 4–23). Contrary to flimsy construction and quick depreciation of current buildings, the framework would be amortized over a much longer period. Such an approach represents prudent use of available resources and, despite the increased initial costs, will result in savings in the long run.

Figure 4–22
A view of the model framework from the southwest. Note: Because of the abstract nature of the model, absence of signs of life, recognizable details, and cultural precedent, such manmade cliffs are perhaps awe-inspiring, but they must communicate permanence and protection.

Figure 4-23
The Nandaimon gate of Todaiji temple in Nara, Japan, dating from the 1199 reconstruction. Note: The gate was built from standardized construction components by using exposed column penetrating ties. Priority was given to structural beauty and directness in expression. Only extreme conditions, such as earthquakes, fires, and total neglect necessitate complete reconstruction in Japanese architecture. Building parts are replaced when worn out, thus preserving continuity. Achieving similar economies and timelessness in the design of frameworks should be possible.

CONDITION 7: EXPOSURE TO SUNLIGHT

The position of space lots must be determined by the best possible exposure to sunlight.

Why. This requirement is no different from that of apartment buildings and is further reinforced by incorporation of outside garden areas (Figure 4-24). A dwelling that never gets exposed to sunlight is indeed deprived.[6]

How. A house on a private lot provides the greatest choice in exposure: Rooms may be lighted from two or even three directions. Achieving the same exposure in a high-density structure is not possible unless such a structure has a single-loaded corridor or numerous openings in the structure for cross penetration of sunlight. A double-loaded framework should face east and west to offer the greatest exposure. A framework facing south should be single-loaded, as exclusively facing north in the temperate zones of the Northern Hemisphere is generally undesirable. The semi-open core framework, however, offers many other advantages over solidly packed and enclosed housing structures: The interior is likely to be naturally lighted; there are the occasional views of the landscape on the other side; and during early and late hours of the day there will even be direct sunlight from the other side[7] (Figures 4-25 and 4-26).

Figure 4-24
Detail view from the northeast of an early study model showing an unbuilt-on framework with landscape modules for small trees.

Figure 4-25
Apartments within the model framework under late morning sum. (Gary Day, University
of Oregon, 1974.)

Figure 4-26
Apartments in the model framework under winter afternoon sun. Note: Unexpected and often unprogrammable sun penetration from the other side will contribute to the amenities of the interior streets and the space lots. (Gary Day, University of Oregon, 1974.)

CONDITION 8: CHOICE IN SPACE-LOT SIZE

The framework must provide choice in space-lot size.

Why. People do not all need the same size house, nor do all people have the financial means to acquire and maintain extensive dwellings.

How. There are eight different sized space lots in the arrangement of the framework shown in Figures 4–27 and 4–28. In addition to the typical lots, the uppermost, those on grade, and the end lots permit further variations. The smallest space lots between the cuboctahedra (see Figures 4–1 and 4–2) accept more than a modestly sized dwelling to allow for some expansion or change; the largest space lots within the cuboctahedra could eventually contain a dwelling that is the size of a Victorian home. These large space lots could also be subdivided into two space lots by an intermediate floor (Figures 4–1 and 4–2).

Figure 4–27
East elevation of the small and large space lots of the model framework that are next to the ground.

Figure 4-28
West elevation of the small and large space lots of the model framework that are next to the ground.

CONDITION 9: ACCESS NETWORKS

The access networks must allow for delivery of materials to space lots and for removal of bulky items.

Why. Apartment building hallways are minimal connectors that barely allow for moving in of furniture (Figure 4-29). Grand pianos often cannot be fitted through the tight stairs and openings. If the framework is to allow for expansion and change over a long period of time or, conversely, for activities that result in large possessions, such as boats or works of art, the access ways must be sufficiently wide and strong to accept these loads. They should also be able to accommodate space-lot infil building materials, small trees, soil, and other items traditionally confined to outside areas without disruptive consequences.

How. Access networks can be viewed as extensions of urban circulation systems. In the framework shown in Figure 4-30, they are open-air pedestrian "streets," and their position is defined by the structure and the space-lot locations. The gap between the space lots and the streets contributes to social interaction and assures identity and potential articulation of the access system in response to its requirements. The streets are sufficiently wide and high to assure movement of bulky loads. A large service elevator or direct connection with grade of a sloping site can provide the vertical connection. Cars, motorcycles, and campers should not be allowed in the framework due to the detrimental consequences: People again would be endangered and their activities squeezed off the streets.

Figure 4-29

A corridor in a walk-up apartment building (Figure 1-9) in Eugene, Oregon. Note: The windows face into the open to the air hallway, and their curtains are always drawn. A blinding light at the end of the corridor silhouettes the inhabitants.

Figure 4-30
The core structure of the model framework with internal pedestrian streets and stairs from north. Note: These streets are 10′ to 15′ wide and able to support small battery powered vehicles for moving of materials.

CONDITION 10: SOCIAL INTERACTION

The access networks must allow for and facilitate social interaction.

Why. If the framework is to be more than a depository for space lots and to attain desirable qualities as a whole, the access systems must provide an environmental experience comparable with better examples of pedestrian streets of the two-dimensional town. Human beings depend on society for their very survival. The needs of children, adolescents, adults, and the elderly differ considerably, and the public places in the framework should provide for their needs (Figure 4–31).

How. There is no way that the framework can duplicate all the amenities of public access on ground. The framework shown in Figure 4–32, however, has other opportunities seldom possible in ground-based environments. The open space between the interior pedestrian streets and the space lots and the terraced accessways permits visual and audio contact between the street levels. The frequency of stairs puts neighboring levels in easy reach. Various widenings in the street configuration and the change in direction allow for seating, play areas, or other events out of the way of circulation. The gaps between the space lots admit natural light to the interior streets and provide views and a sense of orientation to the outside. The arrangement of cuboctahedral volumes also brings the largest space lots in contact with two circulation levels.

Figure 4–31
Children in Manhattan, Kansas. Note: Of course, copying the public street is impossible, but circulation systems in housing frameworks will have different and unique opportunities for play and other forms of interaction. The designers of the frameworks should facilitate occasion for diverse street life for the young and old.

Figure 4–32
A view of an internal pedestrian street at the jog in the direction of this walkway in the model framework. Note: Out-of-the-way widenings would accomodate gathering places, rest and play areas, and street furniture.

5

The Model Framework–An Example of User-Controlled Environment

The two previous chapters attempted to introduce some of the conditions prerequisite to user-completed, high-density housing. We have begun to outline the more rudimentary aspects of frameworks—fragments of the townframe—and to establish general principles essential to evolution of such environments. The question that must be answered more fully here is: What impact would the presence of such frameworks have on the environment and the lives of people?

We should remember that *framework* means not only the physical structure and the supporting facilities but its more inclusive interpretation as a frame of reference. In this respect we are really after the underlying order and the essential design principles. The concretized framework then is not only a structure but the physical manifestation of this order.

METHODS AND CONSIDERATIONS

Before we can focus on the above question, a brief description of the methods used and the attitudes shaping this study is in order.

In the absence of an existing program and only few developed precedents for user-controlled, -completed, and -adapted housing frameworks, a design probe is the quickest way of getting at the issues related to such habitats. Design by its very nature is integrative. It requires making value judgments and establishing priorities, and it transcends mere assemblage of isolated patterns. A design proposal then can be assessed, further criteria established, and the proposal or parts of it recycled. Although several such clearly identifiable cycles are discernible, in practice the evaluation and adjustment is also continuous. Some parts get redesigned hundreds of times. Recycling, likewise, is not limited to a single project nor the work of one individual or group. Past endeavors constitute departure points for future experiments.

The design of the study framework was preceded by projects with architectural design students at the University of Oregon (Figures 5–1 and 5–2). Although much less ambitious, they provided some valuable insights. In a more continuous way, the students have used this author's work as a basis for their explorations, as many of the illustrations in this volume attest. Intermittent studio projects focused on parallel issues at other scales.

Not only must the most nagging questions be answered, but the amenities of living within these

Figure 5-1
A space-lot framework of walk-up height with two-story capacity within each volume (also see Figure 4-3). Note: The volume above the delicatessen was filled in by a student unfamiliar with architecture in order to simulate user adaptation more closely. This kind of user-controlled framework could fit comfortably and incrementally in similar scale neighborhoods (Bryan Croeni, University of Oregon, 1972.)

housing frameworks have to be simulated as convincingly as possible. Design is, after all, a rehearsal of reality. The more complete it is, the more easily we can evaluate its impact, its advantages, and its disadvantages and then make improvements and progress beyond the conceptual. The project described in this volume is only beginning to do that. Sketches, montages, and photographs of models place us within such habitats and either reinforce our fears or assure us that life in these contexts is not only possible but hopefully even desirable.

Instead of recognizing the recurring patterns, both man ordered and natural, we latch on to the unique site. If there is a choice in site location, we will likely pick the place by the river, rather than, for example, the repetitive, commonplace block. Given a neighborhood of residential streets, we may center our attention on that special tree or old house. Such easily recognizable amenities limit and channel the design task and thus make it easier. However, while these are not unimportant, initially focusing on unique features will obscure the prevailing structure of the built environment. We may very well end up with a supportive place, but its contribution to other similar building needs could be, at best, incidental.

In view of our exponentially deteriorating environment and the scarcity of sensitive designers, design strategies are needed that would extend beyond the problems of a particular site. Focus on characteristic systems and existing patterns not only affects the entire site but may, in fact, have wider application. Special features, then, can mold and shape more general patterns and culminate in a place unlike any other. The danger of monotony does not exist because of the variety of natural and manmade patterns and their infinite combinations and potential articulation.

The design of the study framework has gone even a step beyond. It originated without a definite site. In an attempt to get at the optimal relationships between the space lots, their orientation in relation to sun, and the assumption of a moderate climate (the Pacific Northwest) was the only context (Figures 5-3 to 5-14). In this respect the method used is no different from Le Corbusier's Radiant City and his Unite d'Habitation.[1] The patterns of a particular site not only test the prototype, but, furthermore, require adaptations and transformations. The abstract becomes concrete and the universal, unique. The traditional architectural design process is a simultaneous development of theoretical models together with their specific application in a precise ecological and cultural context, but the very complexity of the task required this more linear approach from the general to the particular.

Although an environment on the scale of megastructures must integrate all aspects of human existence, the intention during the design phase of the

(Text continued on page 97.)

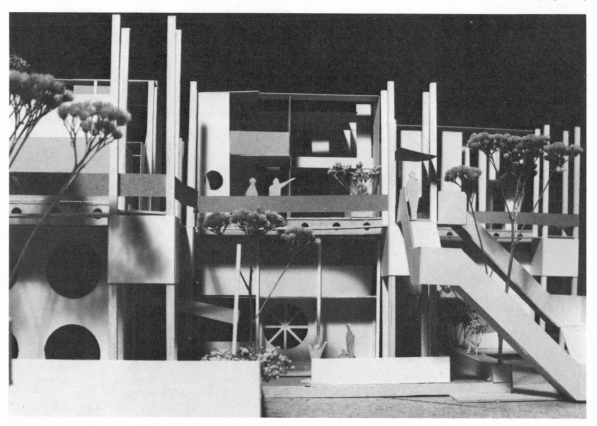

Figure 5-2
A detailed view of the dwelling space lots in a walk-up framework (shown in Figure 5-1). (Bryan Croeni, University of Oregon, 1972.)

Figure 5-3
An early study model of a portion of a high-density user-adapted housing framework. Note: The east elevation shows space lots that have not yet been built on. The scheme was revised because there was insufficient variation in space-lot size and some of the volumes were too dark. The model was taped and retaped, perhaps as many as thirty times during the search for optimum space-lot relationships.

Figure 5-4
Revised version of the preliminary study model of a portion of the framework from the northeast showing space lots that have not yet been built on. Note: The louvers are token privacy barriers that were studied at a later time.

Figure 5-5
Revised version of the preliminary study model of a portion of the framework from the southwest showing space lots that have not yet been built on.

Figure 5-6

Plan of a typical unoccupied portion of the model framework at the sixth street level. Note: This recurring part does not show the vertical circulation core. Terracing of the south side discloses the lower space lots.

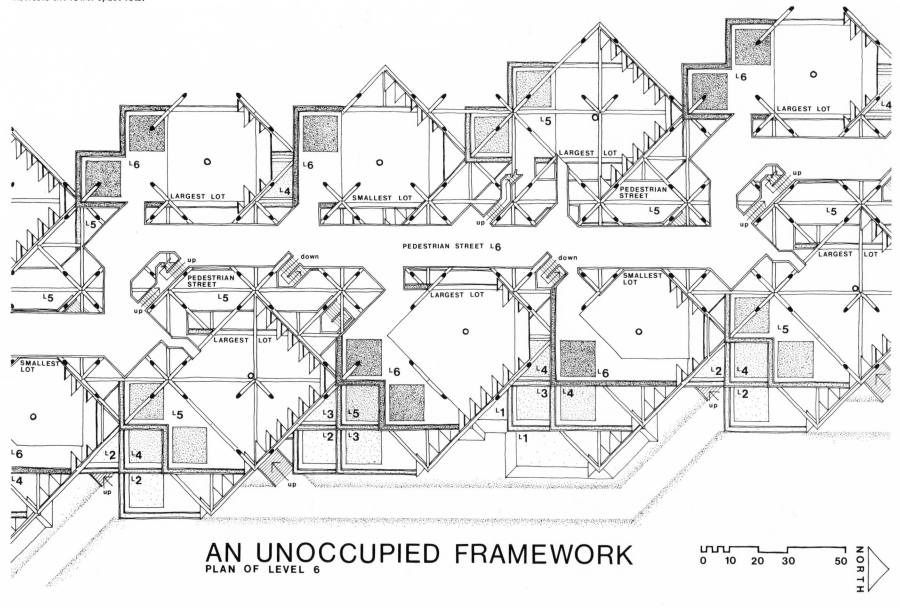

AN UNOCCUPIED FRAMEWORK
PLAN OF LEVEL 6

Figure 5-7
Plan of a typical occupied portion of the model framework at the sixth street level. Note: Some of the stairs have been extended to provide special platforms. No attempt was made to show dwellings that drastically depart from today's residential environments. The geometry of the space lots would, however, influence room layouts and spatial arrangements. Such residential frameworks can easily accept small offices, as well as people with alternative lifestyles. Each dwelling has its own heating system, chosen by the owner.

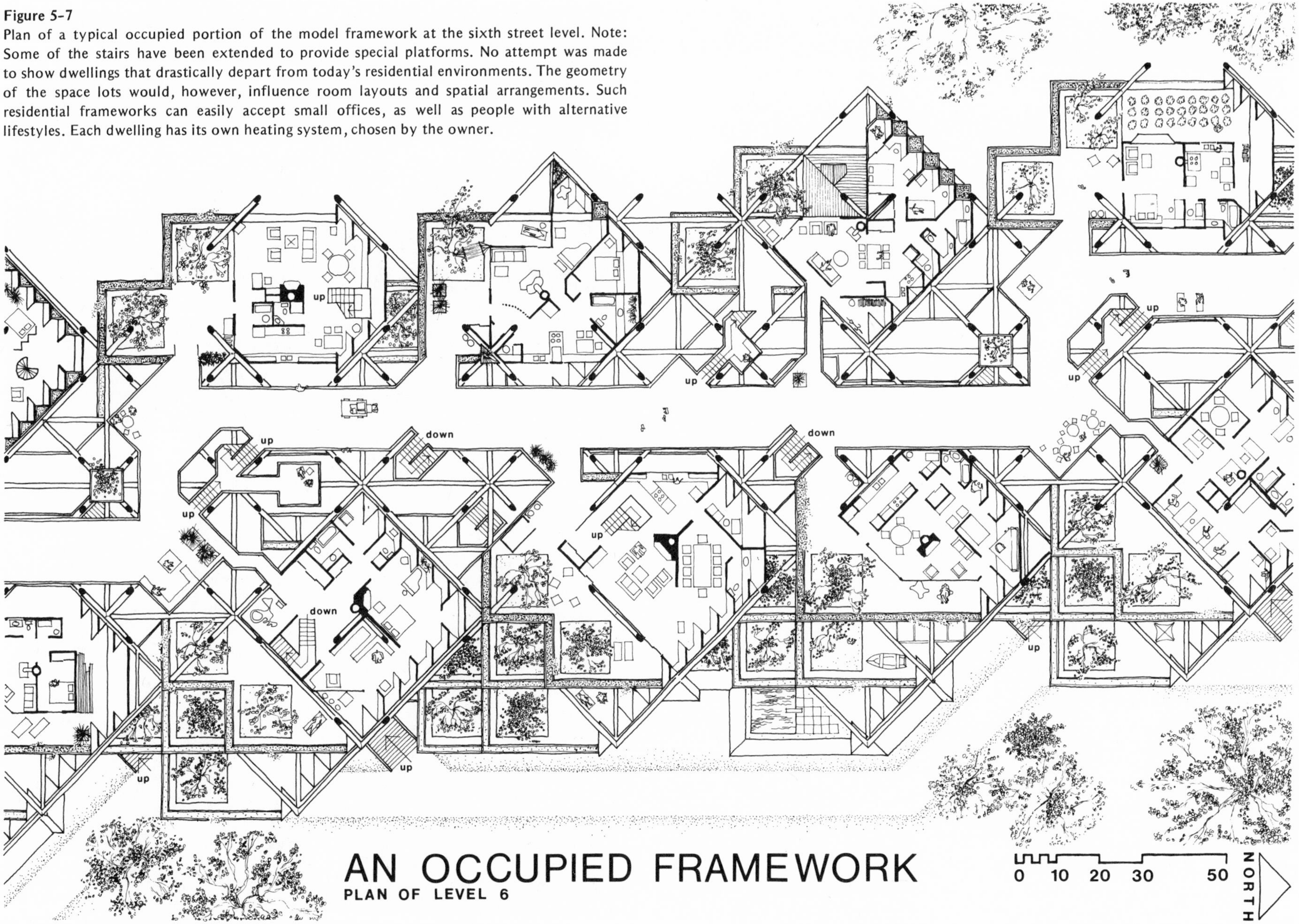

AN OCCUPIED FRAMEWORK
PLAN OF LEVEL 6

0   10   20   30   50

NORTH

Figure 5-8
The east side of the unoccupied framework from above. Note: Penthouse-like space lots at the top permit skylights, higher gardens, or other departures from the prevailing system. Sloping surfaces could easily accommodate solar collectors, and wind generators could extend from the structure. Tent membranes will eventually cover the upper pedestrian street.

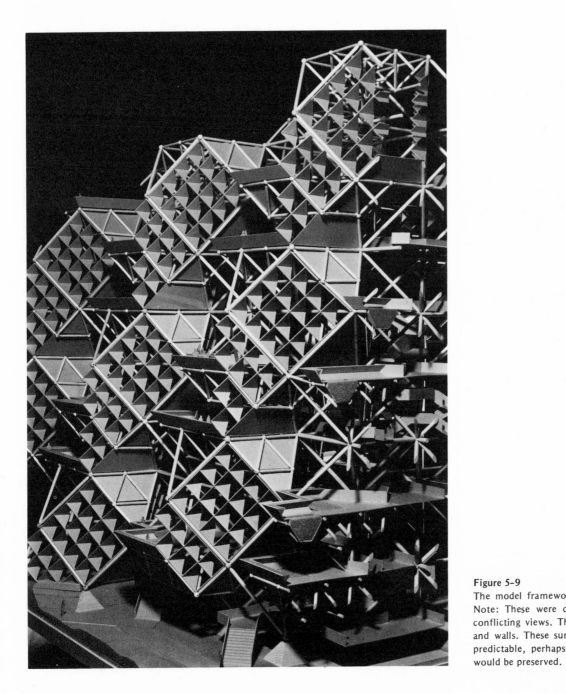

Figure 5-9
The model framework from the northeast showing the brise-soleil-type of privacy barriers. Note: These were designed to allow maximum light and sun penetration, yet screen out conflicting views. The apex of the pyramidal surfaces line up for orderly joining to floors and walls. These surfaces contribute to the strong visual sense of order. In view of the unpredictable, perhaps even chaotic filling in of the framework, the clarity of the structure would be preserved.

Figure 5-10
A view of the unoccupied model framework from the southwest.

The Model Framework—An Example of User-Controlled Environment

Figure 5-11
Detail view of the unoccupied framework from the southwest. Note: This side provides more sheltered space lots and a setting previously impossible with rectilinear structures. The wide railings with planters give a feeling of security in the open gardens and prevent the residents from looking down onto the private lower gardens of others.

Figure 5-12
Section of the unoccupied model framework (looking south).

Figure 5-13
East elevation of the unoccupied model framework. Note: This particular application of the exploded cuboctahedral structure ranges in height from fourteen to eighteen stories with approximately ten feet per story.

Figure 5-14
West elevation of the unoccupied model framework.

The Model Framework—An Example of User-Controlled Environment

project was to develop a framework or context for personal shelters that would not be dependent on small shops and cafes for its very existence. The point is well made by Alison and Peter Smithson[2] that we should be able to design livable housing without relying on commercial facilities. Boutiques and sidewalk cafes throughout the framework cannot be supported unless there is an influx of outsiders. The presence of such shops is, of course, desirable and in some special places essential, but the frequency of occurrence of these facilities does not justify their continuous incorporation. Nothing should prevent integration of shops, offices, and even small production plants, but housing cannot be contingent on the presence of these activity-generating functions. Horizontal shopping and entertainment streets can be integrated in the framework either on the lower or some other floor—wherever the community would be best served. The students' projects in this study centered these activity-generating facilities around the vertical circulation cores (Figures 5-15 and 5-16).

If the user is to exercise a measure of control over his immediate environment, such control can only take place within a reference frame. A framework establishes limits through its inherent capacities, and it determines the range and nature of experience (Figure 5-17). It precludes alternatives at some scales, and its very existence permits infinite variations in others. The framework is the indispensable basis of high-density user-adapted housing and the determinant of architectural and urban form and

space. The various specific conditions for the existence of such housing were described in Chapter 4.

Certainly, there is no one ultimate framework for user-controlled housing. The need exists for countless variations of such frameworks. The physical and cultural context should be the primary determinant of the nature and configuration of the framework. Urban or rural setting, predominant building forms, climate, terrain, social patterns, population pressures should be among the key factors considered in the design of the framework. Invariably, the height and density of the framework must be the consequence of the context.

Adaptable housing can and must exist in all scales.

At present the individual house still does permit some choice and change (although often in a frustrating way), but the adaptability of available dwellings decreases with increase in density. If we believe that the "man's home is his castle" mind set still has validity, then how do we translate this into megascale frameworks? How do we live in the modern "beehive" and retain a measure of identity? These questions demand answers. Examination of historical examples reveals that the problems of density have been with us since the dawn of civilization. With change in our attitude towards design of housing, that there are infinite variations in scale and form of user-developed housing will become apparent. The more examples become

Figure 5-15
A detail study of the intersection of vertical and horizontal circulation systems of the model framework (see also Figure 5-18). Note: Service and passenger elevators connect the interior streets to plazas and a service road below. An occasional store, restaurant, and so forth, not necessarily at every intersection, would serve the inhabitants. Some of the pedestrian streets terminate in open walks and observation platforms to take advantage of a view. (Steve Abbot and Robert Pare, University of Oregon, 1974.)

Figure 5-16
Detail view of central stairs and platforms at the intersection of three wings of the model framework with cafe, outside eating areas, and fountains. Note: Many of the internal pedestrian streets terminate on the steep grade. The elevator core is not visible in the photograph. (Peter Alef and John Sonderen, University of Oregon, 1974.)

Figure 5-17
Interior of the largest space lot on the west side of the model framework (looking north). Note: The cuboctahedral volume can be subdivided into two two-story space lots by inserting a permanent floor above the interior truss members. The structural components also define the legal boundaries of the lot, thus making visualizing the available space possible. The change in floor height communicates the limits of enclosure, thereby assuring an outdoor area.

available, the more convincing will be this approach towards housing and the greater will be the choice to the inhabitants.

For medium densities, designing user-adapted housing analogous with prevailing lower-density building types—such as row houses, walk-up apartments, and various cluster schemes similar to planned unit developments—is relatively easy. Such frameworks do not need to resort to complex structural and spatial systems (Figures 5–1 and 5–2). User-developed, low-rise space lots would fulfill housing requirements of a considerable part of urbanized areas throughout the world where close proximity to land is still possible.

The dominant high-rise buildings, such as tower and slab-type apartments, are ill suited for user-adapted housing, not to mention their undesirable social and psychological effects. Their development was brought about by innovation in structure, building techniques, and vertical movement systems. The architect often has little control over the housing types. Their height per se is not what is undesirable, but rather the inherent isolation of the buildings, which results in arbitrary compositional arrangement of blocks. Furthermore, these shapes make incorporation of outside garden areas, horizontal and diagonal connections, and movement of materials for future changes next to impossible. Incremental growth both of the framework and within the individual space lots, as well as adaptation to landscape, is equally difficult to achieve. Man is at the mercy of building technology and established stereotype concepts of mass housing.

The purpose of this study was to focus on high-density user-adapted housing and to generate alternatives to prevailing high-rise buildings. The need for high-density housing was based on the following assumptions:

High-density living furthers social interaction and contributes to man's intellectual and emotional growth;

Available urban land is limited by service boundaries, preservation of agricultural land, and reservation of flood plains, wildlife habitats, and forest lands;

Density of urban areas must be structured to allow for three-dimensional transformation instead of the conventional two-dimensional suburban sprawl.

The framework illustrated in Figures 5–6 to 5–14 is a megascale fragment of a townframe—that is, a section of an ongoing structure and only one manifestation of the many possible heights and configurations of this particular geometry. Many other ordered and random ways of structuring this framework can be accomplished by using the same exploded order of the cuboctahedra (Figures 5–18 and 5–19). The "saturated" geometry can be "sliced" in many different ways: The structure can climb as steeply as in the illustrated model or in several very shallow angles. A considerable number of variations in plan, height, width, and slope are possible, thereby facilitating adaptation on and integration in the landscape as suggested by some of the student projects. The framework can be single or double loaded and ground hugging; it can also enclose large internal spaces if both sides are terraced similar to the eastern side of this model. The nature and location of the internal circulation system and the outside decks would, of course, change with the change of the configuration.

The design of the framework was based on the assumption that by focusing on the most complex and demanding conditions first—namely, high-density housing—not only more innovative low-density housing may emerge but perhaps some of the prejudices against high-density living in the United States could be minimized. The absence of a particular context forces the designer to respond to the inherent characteristics of the framework only; the site cannot be used as an excuse for failure to consider the essential relationships between the space lots. Capricious decisions become conspicuous. This approach must assure the adaptability of the framework to a particular site and its usability in incomplete stages, as well as safeguard the possibility that users' personal whims and happy accidents will have an opportunity to manifest themselves and eventually humanize the framework.

THE ROLE OF GEOMETRY

Building is inconceivable without geometry: A building may be geometrically describable or so called "free form," regular or irregular, repetitive or transformed. Geometry is present in every aspect of the physical world, and without some kind of a geometrical description, a design cannot be communicated to the builder and user and the "free form" design may have to be built by the designer.

While in buildings of modest height the role of geometry is often obscured for whatever reason, geometry is the very order that permits conception and execution of complex and extensive structures such as the model framework described in this chapter. Geometry is not only the space-defining order but also the determinant of the structure system and the organizer of the building's functions. It affects every aspect in the design and use of such structures. The choice of geometry is never arbitrary but results from the examination of the inherent characteristics and growth patterns of the space defining units.

Early in the design of the framework we found that rectilinear geometry would not satisfy the demanding requirements of the proposal. The incorporation of outside garden areas, with provisions for landscape modules on both sides of the framework, and the steep ascent of the structure, which avoids a dark underside and a large interior volume, become possible only because of triangulated geometry. A rectilinear framework would result in a bending-

The Model Framework—An Example of User-Controlled Environment

resistant structure, which by its very nature would be extremely bulky and prohibitively expensive. In fact, this author does not know of any proposal that can climb virtually vertically yet incorporate comparable amenities.

Hitherto, sloping structures have been either dependent on terrain or have ended up with rather depressing undersides, as in Kikutake's tiered housing proposals.[3] Incorporation of shops in these areas below the residences would make housing contingent on presence of such facilities.

Use of rectilinear geometry for terrace housing also requires a forest of columns to support it. Housing proposals with terraces on both sides are initially very appealing. However, the resulting large interior space is difficult to put to use. It is out of scale with the more intimate character of residential environment and overpowering to the few play areas and communal facilities generally shown in such proposals.

The need to give identity to and to avoid horizontal and vertical stratification of the space lots; the necessity of a substantial "street" for movement of materials, service, and access; the desirability of contact between several street and space-lot levels; the requirement of light, air, and occasional sunlight in the interior; the need for glimpses of the outside from the street were some of the other requirements instrumental in the choice of the geometry. The space truss structure with its point supports is also easiest on the landscape. Piers can be eliminated in difficult terrain, openings can be "carved out" in the framework, and

the multitude of alternative configurations and transformations promise optimum integration of natural and manmade environments. The requirements that led to the design of this framework were discussed in greater detail in Chapter 4.

The geometric order of the model framework consists of exploded cuboctahedra (Figures 5-20 and 5-21), with the space between the cuboctahedra defined by tetrahedra and octahedra that are geometrically related to the cuboctahedra (Figure 5-22). In this arrangement every one of the six square and eight triangular surfaces of a cuboctahedron is equidistant from the surrounding cuboctahedra. The edge of a cuboctahedron (thirty feet long) equals and defines

Figure 5-19 (above)
Part of the framework of Betsy Barsamian's and Fred Levy's project for the south hills of Eugene. Note: The framework changes from single to double loaded and even three units wide arrangement with the center used for communal and commercial facilities. The location of the space lots is determined by access to sun and the terrain. (University of Oregon, 1974; from a class taught jointly by the author and Ronald Lovinger of the Department of Landscape Architecture.)

Figure 5-18 (at left)
An intersection of two different applications of the model framework (from the southeast). Note: The configuration on the left is identical to the prototypical double-loaded framework and placed on the north-south axis while the structure on the far right is low, single loaded, and ground hugging to take advantage of the southern exposure. Most of the space lots are still not filled in. (Steve Abbott and Robert Pare, University of Oregon, 1974.)

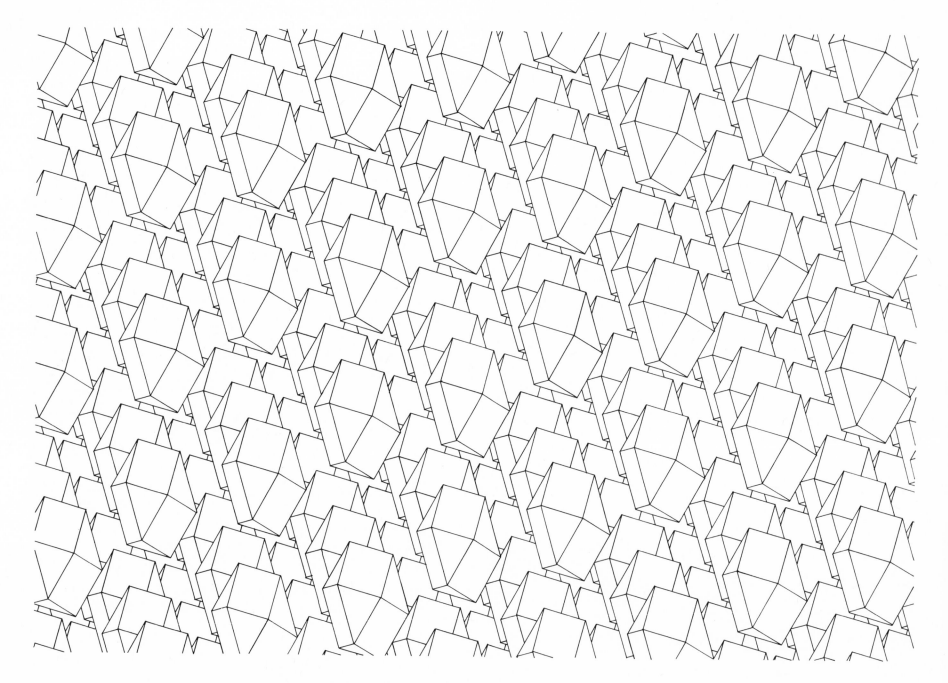

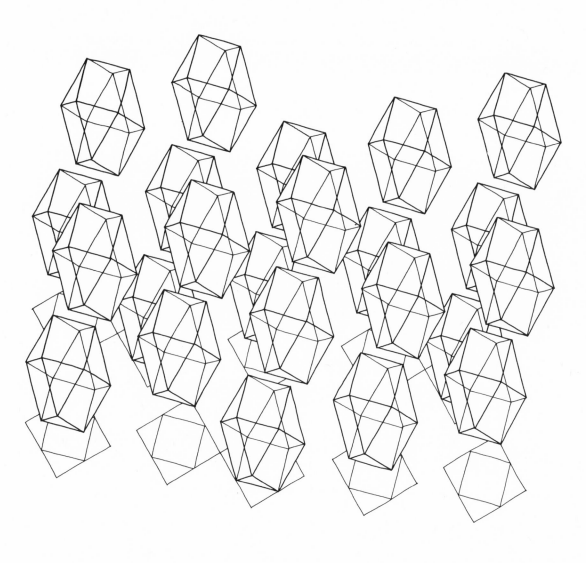

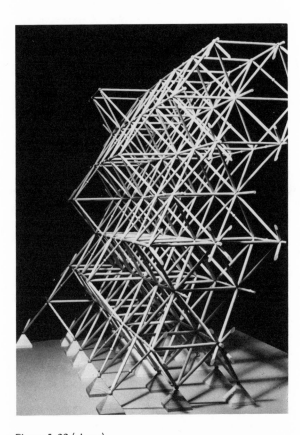

Figure 5-21 (at left)
An axonometric drawing of the exploded cuboctahedra only as used in this fragment of the model framework.

Figure 5-22 (above)
The structure of the internal core between the cuboctahedra in the model framework. Note: The wood beads and dowels were chosen to speed the model-building task and are not necessarily representative of the nature of the actual structure. The spherical connectors suggest steel rather than concrete, which this structure would have to have for reasons of fire safety.

Figure 5-20 (at left)
An axonometric drawing of the "saturated" exploded cuboctahedral module. Note: Frameworks composed of this polyhedra can be "sliced" from this geometrical configuration in all conceivable ways.

The Role of Geometry   103

the distance between the cuboctahedra. The framework can also be visualized as an omnidirectional tetrahedral–octahedral close-packing system with the cuboctahedra carved out and a single layer of tetrahedra-octahedra between two opposite surfaces of the cuboctahedra. The exploded cuboctahedral arrangement thus results in a natural order inherent in this geometry and in a framework that is conceptually infinitely expandable. Any amount or any configuration of this particular arrangement can be used. The model and drawings then represent one application of the framework.

The explosion of the cuboctahedra is analogous to separation of rectangular modules commonly employed in building design. The space between such modules defines the circulation system, the location of mechanical systems, service spaces, or some other function. This clarification of the building's purpose is not only intellectually satisfying, but such spatial zoning contributes to the adaptability of the structure during its duration and, in turn, determines the life cycle of the construction (see Figures 2-26 and 2-27).

The purpose and function of the served spaces can change without major adjustments in the rest of the building. The circulation system is the lifeline to these spaces: Its existence must be assured no matter what. Consequently, it may be articulated through structure and choice of materials. The life span of the circulation system can be further prolonged through integration of mechanical and electrical services in this circulation, which in turn provides easier access to these short-life systems. This arrangement is no different from the relationship between the utilities along our public streets and the served lots, with the exception that we ludicrously place public utilities below the pavement. Every time something goes wrong (and it does so all the time), the street is torn up and traffic is interrupted. Thus to eliminate or interrupt the street itself is a major decision indeed, as it is a lifeline of the surrounding blocks.

Thus the space between the cuboctahedra provides for the access networks and other support systems; yet it recognizes their independence, need for variations, and the inevitability of their transformation over time (Figures 5-23 and 5-24). The exploded cuboctahedra within the tetrahedral–octahedral close-packing arrangement defines the limits of each space lot and assures that light, air, and sun will penetrate

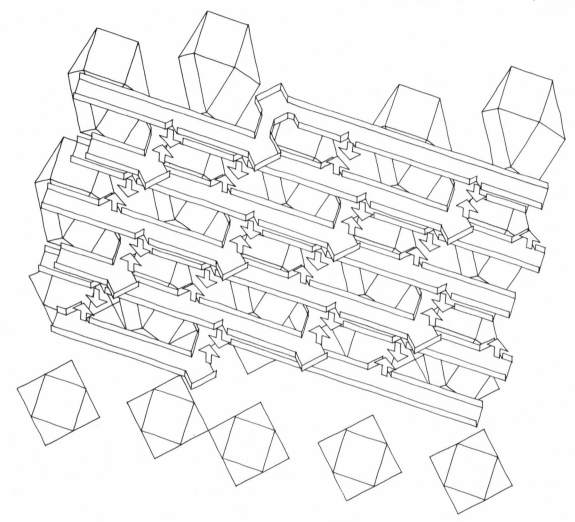

Figure 5-23
An axonometric drawing of the internal pedestrian streets (with stair locations represented by arrows). Note: The cuboctahedra in front has been left off for reasons of clarity.

Figure 5-24
The core structure of the model framework with the internal pedestrian streets and stairs from east. Note: The change in the direction of the streets is inherent in the exploded cub-octahedral geometry between which the streets run and result in the terracing effect. The projections with the missing railings indicate the connections to the gardens of the space lots.

the structure, but the tetrahedral–octahedral infil between the exploded cuboctahedra results in an optimum structural system. Furthermore, the geometrical growth pattern permits easy adaptation to landscape and multiple options within the environment.

The exploded cuboctahedra constitute a conceptual order—an order that could be superimposed over the whole site (Figure 5-20). The framework is only one application of this order (Figure 5-25). Various configurations and spaces can be structured without ever departing from this discipline (Figures 5-26 and 5-27). The system is a highly complex modular one, but the complexity is not arbitrary. It is the result of recognition of the need for spatial separation and service and served spaces that can be further articulated through the identification of many other orders inherent in building construction. This hierarchic order is organic in nature and of greatest significance to the transformation of buildings and environments and the role of the user.

SPACE AND STRUCTURE

There is, no doubt, some initial difficulty in working with such an angular geometry, but there is surprisingly little loss of usable space, particularly within the space lots. The frustrations are mostly related to the design and especially to the difficulties in communicating the architecture generated by polygonal geometry systems, which may account for the limited advances in this area.

The larger the size of the polyhedra, the more usable the space. Although all physical matter constitutes space structures when viewed in microscale, enlargement of microscale geometry to macroscale structures has been, with few exceptions, limited to roof structures. Modules on the order of three to five feet are most common. We do not have enough experience with much larger geometries. Tange's "Theme Center" for Expo '70 in Osaka[4] with ten-meter modules is perhaps the best built example, although once again the structure is used for spanning space. The argument that such structures should be used for spanning large spaces only does not hold because we do crawl inside rectilinear geometry. Most buildings above several stories in height are space frames either of the close-packing type or linear or planar vertical cantilevers. If other geometries embody properties that the rectilinear lacks, there is no reason why we cannot do likewise. The application of such geometries in megastructures has been proposed by Yona Friedman,[5] Eckhard Schulze-Fielitz,[6] and others. In fact, the firm of Affleck, Desbarats, Dimakopoulos, Lebensold and Sise, Architects, designed the most demanding space truss megastructure hitherto conceived and built: the "Man the Producer" theme pavilion for Expo '67 in Montreal[7] (Figures 2-10, 2-11, and 2-35). The advantage of space trusses is clear: No other structure system will accommodate equally complex demands with greater ease.

We could of course use the tetrahedral–octahedral geometry exclusively and "carve out" larger volumes within this matrix. This approach promises the greatest diversity in space lots, yet it requires an enormous amount of design energy: The relationship between each space lot would be different. Thus this method is best reserved for special places and facilities. In the absence of a particular program and other clues for such variations, change in the geometry of the space lots would be arbitrary. Given valid reasons for additional changes in the space-lot size and geometry, such as site conditions and occupancy requirements, gradual transformation or some more abrupt modification should be justifiable. Conflicting conditions, however, would be inevitable and the quality of common interior spaces would be impossible to assure if the size and shape of the space lots were entirely left up to the owners. Eventual spatial needs are not predictable due to circumstances over which we have no control. As the size of the space lot defines the limits of construction and not necessarily the extent of the dwelling, the initial choice as to size or shape is less important than in conventional tightly packed habitats where no future additions are possible.

The need for ambiguity and diversity in the built environment has been recognized.[8] Complexity, however, should result from response to forces and needs, be they physical, psychological, social, or cultural. Initial architect-designed complexity per se beyond what is inherent in the system often results in highly artificial environments. Such an approach mirrors the values of the designer. While this type of effort may well culminate in a work of art, too often attempts to be interesting border on the purely cosmetic and do not reflect lifestyles and ongoing processes. Our roadside developments are perhaps the best examples of this attitude towards building.

The cuboctahedra and the smallest space lots in between constitute the context for manifesting the users' material existence. Choice can be exercised at a scale that is of greatest significance to the inhabitants —that is, within their personal realm. Complexity and diversity will be a natural consequence and the users' prerogative. The occupied framework will reflect the values of the users. It can be as rich and diversified or as dull and repetitive as the inhabitants care to make it. The current housing approach is a virtual guaranty of monotony. Within the framework, however, a vernacular may well develop and trends will be started by those discovering unique ways of using their space lots. The students at the University of

(Text continued on page 110.)

Figure 5-25 (at right)
Plan of the "saturated" exploded cuboctahedral modules (see Figure 5-20) with several possible single- and double-loaded framework arrangements "extracted" from this order.

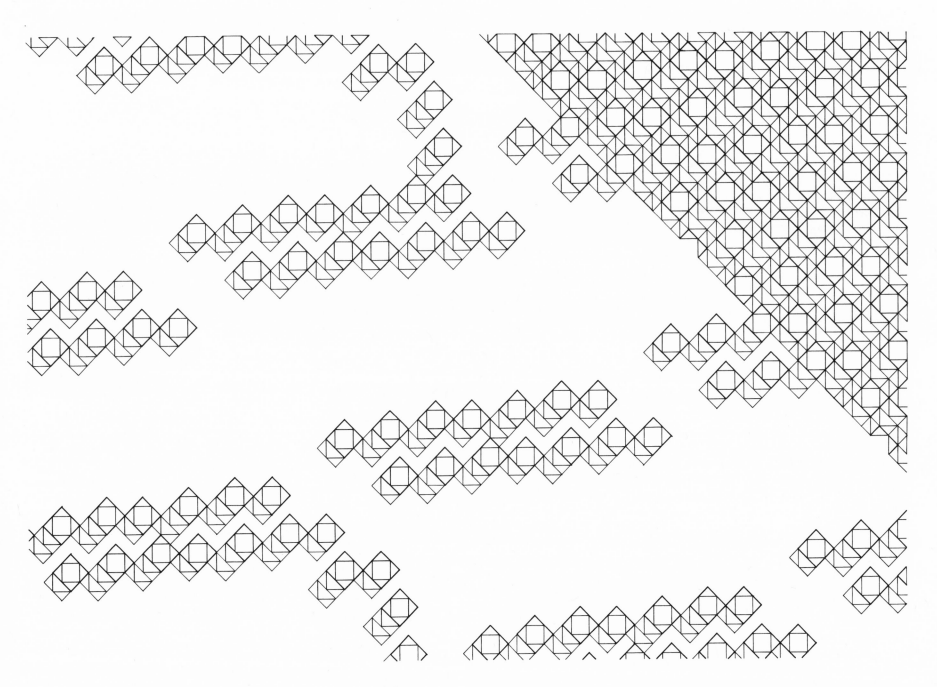

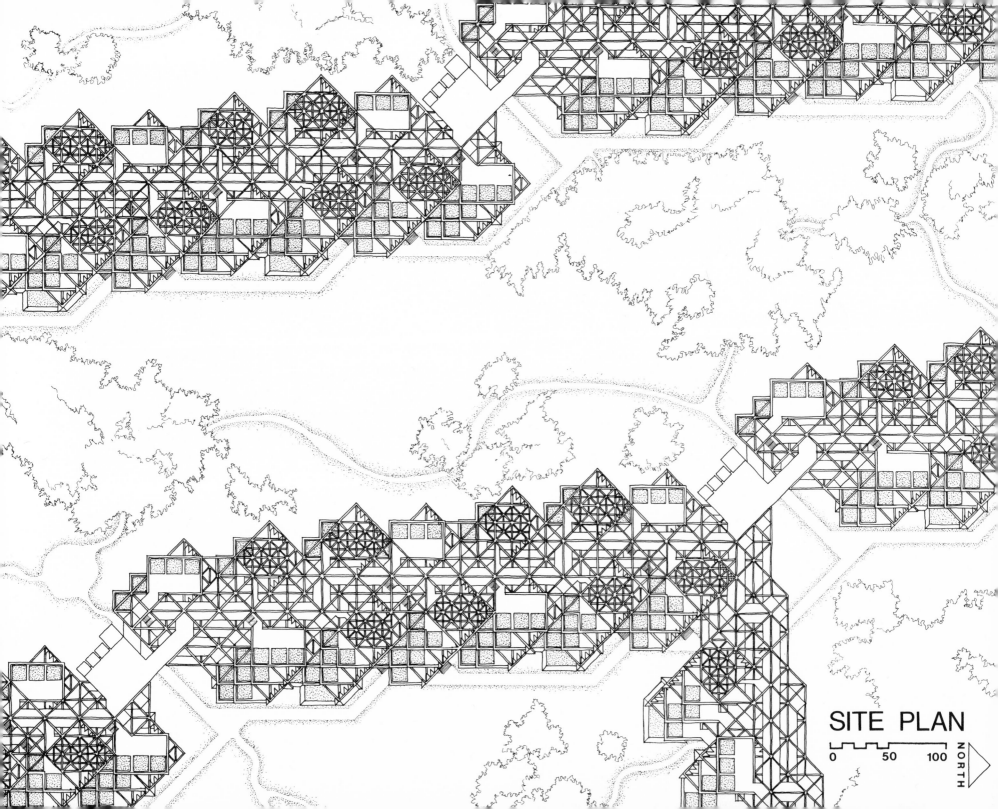

SITE PLAN

0   50   100   NORTH

Figure 5-27
The test of the framework through the design of a community in the south hills of Eugene, Oregon. Note: This student project attempted to integrate the natural patterns with manmade systems. The projected five dwellings per acre would have destroyed the highly sensitive site. The mega-scale framework is comfortably absorbed by the surrounding hills and reaches, at times, even greater heights than those shown in the large model. The model is an abstraction due to the difficulty of realistically representing such frameworks. The framework varies in height, and a single-loaded street system was used on the south facing slopes. (John Linquist, Hossein Torabi, and William Willis, University of Oregon, 1974; from a class taught jointly by the author and Ronald Lovinger of the Department of Landscape Architecture.)

Figure 5-26 (at left)
Site and roof plan of a possible arrangement of an unoccupied framework with a single-loaded pedestrian street variant below. Note: Access drives can be below the structure, thus resulting in minimal disruption of the site. Assuming four people per small space lot and eight per the maximum size lot, one of the framework increments could house over four hundred people with amenities comparable to detached housing.

Oregon who used the model framework as a departure for their own infil give some indication of its use (Figures 5-28, 4-5, 5-29, and 5-30). Neighboring space lots took on similar character (Figure 5-31), and the angular geometry provided useful clues to the use of the space.

Most of the sloping surfaces of the model framework, provided that the space lot is filled in to its limits, occur at the top of the lots. These are somewhat reminiscent of the old houses that are our nineteenth-century heritage. Attics, carriage houses, rooftop apartments, and similar spaces with sloping surfaces are particularly appealing and in continuous demand. We do seem to find comfort in identifying with the past, and the sloping roof is an archetype of shelter for much of mankind.

The angular geometry is a natural consequence of the space truss structure. Attempts to include such sloping surfaces in a rectilinear frame inevitably end up looking forced or have the appearance of tacked-on sheds. No doubt, the full potential of such spaces has yet to be explored, and this project has not progressed far enough to provide a convincing demonstration.

The advantages of the structure system are much clearer. In fact, the space truss is uniquely suitable for large-scale townframes. Through triangulation and pin connections, trusses are designed to transmit axial forces (tension and compression) only in comparison

Figure 5-28
East elevation of the user-completed model framework. Note: No attempts were made to relate the framework to a site, and the lower space lots could not take advantage of proximity to ground due to the fact that all the students were working around the model. There were eight different space lot prototypes because some of the cuboctahedra were subdivided in two; yet the diversity in needs and preferences results in a rich expression that cannot be predetermined by a designer. (University of Oregon class project, 1974.)

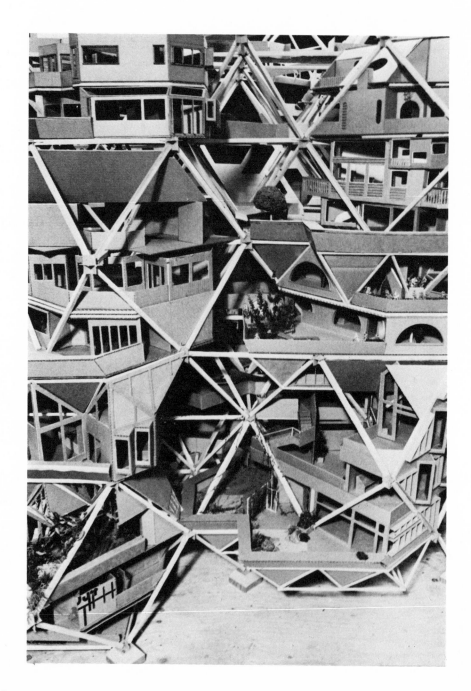

Figure 5-29 (at left)
A detail view from the east of a small balcony outside the attic space trusses under early morning sun. Note: This arrangement demonstrates a sensitive response to the spatial possibilities. (Mohammad Maldjai, University of Oregon, 1974.)

Figure 5-30 (at right)
A detail view from the east of the balcony (shown in Figure 5-29) under late morning sun. (Mohammad Maldjai, University of Oregon, 1974.)

Figure 5-31
Two filled-in space lots of the model framework. Note: The
influence of the use of adjoining space lots and the possible
development of a vernacular architecture is suggested by the
infil of these two volumes. The small space lot (designed
by David Reed) and the upper half of the cuboctahedron
(designed by Gerald Redding) use identical approaches to
space. Both projects use vertical walls between the 15′
module space trusses protruding out in a similar way. Reed's
project started with a small studio apartment on the far
right and additions subsequently filled in this small space
lot. (University of Oregon, 1974.)

to bending-resistant structures that are dependent on material mass and rigid connections. Trusses are perhaps the most efficient and versatile structures for space-lot frameworks. Tension and surface structures are too dependent on form and more restrictive in cellular buildings. Space trusses are also about the safest structures available for resisting seismic and wind loads due to their geometric stability and alternate routes of load transmission. Local failures may not necessarily affect the stability of the entire structure.

Le Corbusier's pilotis notwithstanding, many buildings still are impenetrable barriers for man and natural systems alike. Load-bearing walls or solidly filled-in frames with the ground floor fully utilized virtually destroy any remnants of natural patterns. Consequently, design with nature is difficult, and man's contribution is less likely to end up being complimentary. There is no building that would not alter the site conditions, but the space truss framework with its point supports permits penetration of drainage, vegetation, and wildlife patterns. If site conditions so require, some of the piers can even be eliminated more easily than in other structure systems, with the framework bridging over ravines or opening up vistas, and the model framework can be built more easily on a sloping terrain because the piers can be placed at different elevations.

The structure of the model framework would be assembled from precast concrete members that can vary in cross-section according to their task. Hitherto, space trusses by and large have been built of steel, aluminum, or laminated wood. None of these are safe against fire, and fireproofing of steel does not make much sense due to the complexity of the geometry. In isolated instances precast and prestressed concrete trusses and space trusses have been used with great success.[9] They have, however, been too small in scale and extent to take full advantage of the material. The details would have to be worked out, but the members could be directly bolted together much like Neal Mitchell's preengineered, precast concrete frame, with the bolts in turn fireproofed.[10]

The advantage of space trusses in general is that removing and replacing members is easy. If the need arises, the structure can be extended, damaged components replaced, lighter members substituted with heavier ones, or the geometry rearranged for whatever reason. Given reasonable care and control during design and production, the framework would be a kit that has the potential to remain supportive for centuries if not millenia. With minor changes, it can conceivably accommodate a multitude of human endeavors. A computer program, not only on the structural design but on all other systems as well, could remain in effect to assist with the changes during the lifetime of the framework. Ability to renew itself must be inherent in a structure for user-developed housing, and the space truss permits this better than any other structure system.

The structure, as well as all other physical systems, must be explicit. People and children particularly like to know what holds a building up, where the rainwater goes, how the elevators operate, or what happens to the garbage.

The natural and manmade environment is a school: An understanding of surroundings contributes to a bond between man and his habitat. We feel uneasy and threatened by what we don't understand, and our first reaction is to reject it. This human characteristic is particularly true in regard to our response to structure. The presence of visible structure is reassuring.

The structure is the most permanent part of the model framework. Without it, the space lots cannot exist (Figures 5-32 and 5-33). Consequently, the structure must communicate permanence and a sense of continuity. No doubt, improvements will be made on the structure as our understanding and techniques change, or it may even become a ruin, but the structure is the visible reference frame through space, as well as time. Lovingly cast and assembled members, like ancient timbers in Japanese architecture or the stones of Rome, can bind man to other epochs and people and events long past.

THE LIFE WITHIN

When we look for a place to live we begin by searching for the ultimate. Immediately we are faced with many contradictions, and inevitably we have to settle for some compromise, if indeed a place is available at all. The hope that we will be able to put down roots and prosper in a place of our choice is, nevertheless, ever present.

Attachment to a shelter is contingent on passage of time and of course ability to possess the place. Parting from a house where we grew up, loved, raised children, and celebrated life is difficult. People, however, are forced to relocate because their apartment or house becomes too small or too big to maintain. There is no room for children or grandparents, the hoped-for shop, or guest room. Moving to another city due to change of jobs or for some other reason results in unavoidable parting with a familiar house, but at least people should not be forced out of a house because it cannot accommodate their space needs.

Thus, the framework space lots should be sufficiently large in size to accommodate future growth and change. Fixing the size of the occupiable volumes is not possible at this time, if indeed it ever will be. Spatial demands vary considerably within the United States alone: Houses in Texas are very large compared to New England, for example.

Obviously not everyone has the need or the means to invest in the largest available space lots. Older couples and confirmed singles will most likely require less space than families or the well-to-do; yet even the smallest space lots should be able to grow from the most minimal cabin-size dwelling to something

Figure 5-32
A section of the model structure with the interior pedestrian streets and stairs only (looking north).

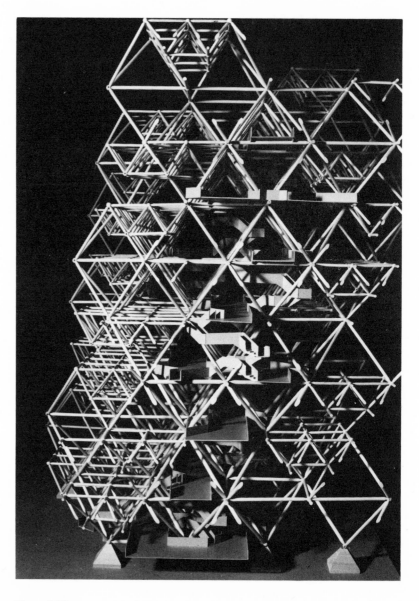

Figure 5-33
A section of the model structure with the interior pedestrian streets and stairs only (looking south).

approximating a two-bedroom apartment. People cannot anticipate their future space needs, but even within the most modest size "house," they should be able to add a library, family room, or a small greenhouse.

The largest space lots in the framework, on the other hand, should eventually be able to accommodate an extended family and shelter a mansion-size dwelling. Once again, these may start out as limited amounts of enclosed space and over the years grow into Victorian-size homes. Investment in a maximum space lot is basically no different from the purchase of a large lot of land. Not to build in the space-lot volume is also the owner's prerogative, in which case the space lot is left undeveloped and held as investment property only. An occasional empty lot properly protected can become a children's playground, but if there are too many such vacant space lots, the surrounding neighborhood suffers from underpopulation. The builder of the framework must recover the investment and the operating authority must collect service and maintenance charges regardless of what the owners do with their space lots.

The tendency to fill in the enclosable volume completely in order to get the maximum return on the initial investment is also most likely. Conceivably, parts of a space lot would be sold off as separate parcels (Figure 5–34). The majority of filled-in areas, however, should grow with the increases in family size and means over an extended period, thereby contributing to the richness of the environment (Figures 5–35 to 5–38). Occasionally some of the construction

Figure 5–34
A view from the southeast of the simulated infil of space lots in the model framework. Note: The "owner" of this complete cuboctahedron decided to fill it in with three rentable apartments; the upper two each have an outside balcony, and the more substantial garden area is reserved for the lower apartment. The apartment complex has its own internal stair exposed to the elements. (Gary Day, University of Oregon, 1974.)

Figure 5-36 (at right)
First time increment illustrating progressive change within the large space lot shown in Figure 5-35. Note: A modest size A-frame type of dwelling with dormers, balconies, and a "tree" house fulfill initial spatial needs of a family.

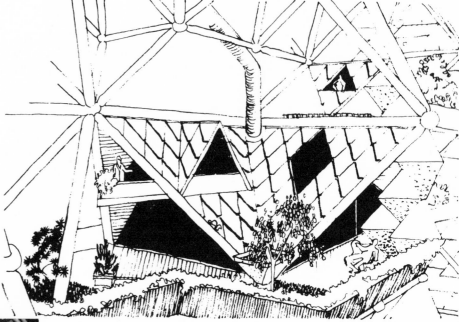

Figure 5-35 (at left)
A view from the southeast of an empty large space lot in the model framework.

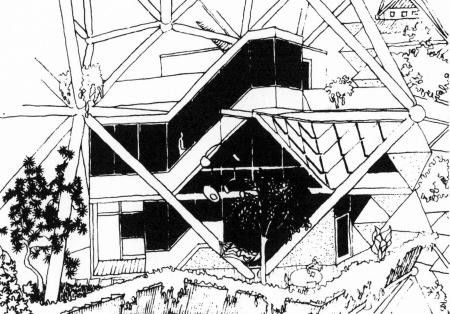

Figure 5-37 (at left)
Second time increment illustrating progressive change within the large space lot shown in Figure 5-35. Note: Additions to the house over the years have expanded the enclosed space.

Figure 5-38 (at right)
Third time increment illustrating progressive change within the large space lot shown in Figure 5-35. Note: Addition of the third floor and other changes have further expanded and enlarged the house, and a large tree has been replaced with a smaller one.

may even be removed: The space lot may burn out or get otherwise damaged or be allowed to deteriorate through some unforeseeable crisis; parts of the space-lot infil system may be returned to the supplier through a default of the purchaser; the new owner may want to put the volume to a completely different use; and so on.

The possibility of growth and change at the scale of the individual dwelling rather than the framework as a whole is what assures the extensive life of user-developed housing and makes adaptation possible. The ability to grow is contingent on extra space (unless expansion is to be towards the outside only) and requires additional structure, access ways, and increased runs in utilities. These, however, establish the context and guarantee this growth. Consequently, a priori determination of precise space-lot size and shape is not only impossible because of the unknown occupants, but unnecessary and undesirable. However, providing a range in space-lot size is necessary and possible, and their adequacy can be tested by simulated use.

In the model framework, the largest available space lots, the complete cuboctahedra, can be subdivided to result in a two-story encloseable space with an outside garden area and a single story with attic space between the trusses and no personal garden space with landscape module capacity (Figure 5-31). The user, of course, can have a garden by not enclosing the entire volume, but this garden can support small trees in portable planters only. Additional variations beyond the eight typical size options shown in this framework could occur at termination of this north-south axis and certainly penthouse-like at the top of the framework. The space lots directly on the ground could easily have larger private garden areas than those higher in the framework.

As in the case of ordinary real estate, the desired size space lot may no longer be available within the framework. The possibility of acquiring neighboring property in such frameworks also exists and will have to be explored further.

The choice of exposure and location is, of course, determined by the particular location and, once again, by what is available. Certain positions undoubtedly will be prime locations because of sun, view, prevailing winds, distance from ground, status, or what have you. The north-south axis assures that at least each side of a double-loaded framework will receive sunlight either in the morning or in the afternoon. In addition there are views through the framework to the other side and, at times, sunlight will penetrate the structure as well (Figure 4-26). What other structure can claim this advantage? The prospective buyers of the space lots should be able to walk through the framework to pick out a desirable location.

If there is one feature of user-completed housing frameworks that is more important than any other and that differentiates such structures from condominiums and terraced housing like Safdie's Habitat,[11] it is the establishment of limits within which the occupants can control their own immediate environment in extent, arrangement, materials, decorations, and so forth. The architecture of condominiums does not recognize and permit any personal manifestation of the user in the form of addition, change, or any other adaptation. Consequently, the boundary of and the space between the space lots are the keys to the design of user-completed housing (Figures 5-39 and 5-40). The definite space between the units—the volume composed of tetrahedra–octahedra between the cuboctahedra—not only provides for the garden areas and access to light and air for the interior streets but assures that the gradual filling in will not result, aesthetically or physically, in awkward, leftover gaps, poor fit, and extreme conflicts in use of space.

If the limits of construction can be defined by structure or other physical elements, the possessable volume can be more easily communicated to the owner or leaseholder of the space lot. Most of the other decisions about the nature of the framework are the result of this initial decision of size, shape, and relationship between the space lots.

The open gap between the space lots and the interior streets with only the structure and the entrance walks bridging between the gaps communicates the limits of construction within each space lot (Figures 5-6 and 5-7). It also gives identity to the individual volumes, permits light, air, and, at times, sun to reach the streets, and assures the openness of the interior. Privacy between the space lots can be achieved by inclusion of louvered or brise-soleil–like surfaces on two sides of the space lots, which eases design decisions as well. Wide and high railings, with the option of a continuous planter within the railing, assure privacy to the garden areas below and also provide a measure of safety (Figures 5-41 and 5-42). Additional safety screens may well be needed in some space lots, particularly those housing children.

In addition to the establishment of limits and rules of construction, allowance must be made for delivery and removal of building materials and other bulky items in a way that does not interfere with the life within. Nor can such delivery and loading be permitted to affect the landscape or create hazards for the inhabitants.

Provisions then for all the processes associated with change and construction must be inherent in the framework. While in some frameworks a traveling overhead crane could be used, a load suspended from a crane will not reach most of the space lots on the west side due to the overhang. Many people also dislike the thought of living in a factory-like structure. Internal access ways sufficiently wide and strong to support small delivery vehicles, such as battery-operated fork-lift trucks were considered most appropriate for this structure.

(Text continued on page 124.)

Figure 5-39
The largest and smallest space lots on the east side of the model framework. Note: The structure, decks, privacy barriers, and railings define the lot, the limits of construction, as well as the extent of gardens. The air space between the space lots guarantees that light will reach the pedestrian streets regardless of the amount of building within these volumes.

Figure 5-40
The largest and smallest space lots on the west side of the model framework.

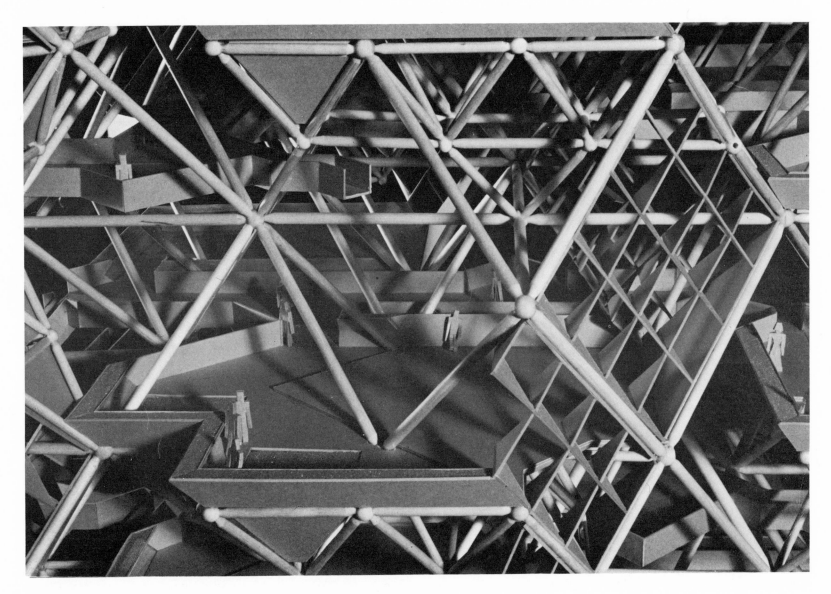

Figure 5-41
Largest unoccupied space lot on the east side of the model framework. Note: The bridge-like connection to the pedestrian street provides a secondary entrance or access to the upper lot if subdivided in two. Change in floor height defines the limit of construction within the lot.

Figure 5-42
Largest unoccupied space lot on the west side of the model framework. Note: The brise-soleil-like surfaces face north and provide privacy between lots. The inhabitants can be as open or closed to the interior pedestrian street as they wish.

Figure 5-43
A typical internal pedestrian street in the model framework prior to occupancy. Note: The streets are 15' wide with 10' width at the narrowest places. Frequently placed stairs facilitate interaction between levels.

Furthermore, the framework must provide clues for design and building and assure safety during construction, regardless of which of the options listed in Chapter 1 the community adopts for the infil. Most of these have yet to be developed for the model framework.

Fortunately, satisfying the most basic requirements for user-completed housing also makes the building much more supportive by automatically providing for opportunities and facilities that should be present in "ordinary" housing. The "internal street,"[12] for example, in addition to carrying materials, is wide enough to provide places where people can gather and children can play. It is a semi-outdoor pedestrian street rather than a dark, endless corridor (Figures 4–29 and 5–43).

The garden area has to perform several functions. It is a transition area between the house and the access way (Figures 5–7 and 4–10), an outside place for contact with the elements and nature, a space for storage, and at times, a construction yard. Direct access from the outside area to the inner street has many advantages: Entrance into the house is more comfortable than directly off the street, and plant and building materials can be more conveniently delivered and stored. In addition to a small entrance garden, the area closest to the street is likely to contain a place for garbage and firewood and a shed for garden equipment, bicycles, baby carriages, and so forth. This connection does not preclude a more direct entrance into the enclosed space or a street-facing porch, which would also be appropriate for a business entrance. The user can have as much or as little contact with the pedestrian street as he prefers. Older people in particular like to sit on the porches and share in the life of the community.

People have different needs and preferences, and the open part of the lot could support diverse activities: Children need sand boxes, pools and play equipment; the barbecuing, which is usually done on the token balconies of apartment houses, as well as garden parties could become part of the social life of the framework community. A boat could be built in the open space, and moving the boat down the inner street and service elevator or ramps would become a communal event. Keeping animals and pets may well be less frustrating than for typical apartment dwellers.

The most important reason for the outside area, however, is man's need for close communion with nature in a whole range of scales: trees, bushes, flowers and butterflies (Figures 5–44 and 5–45). We must be able to feel the breezes and snowflakes and the grass below our feet. Nature is not just what is visible through a picture window or from a balcony; we must be able to relate to it at close range. To celebrate a moment below a tree—albeit modest in size, a tree that has required patient care—is more fulfilling than a remote observance of distant trees and clouds. Day-to-day awareness of nature's pro-

Figure 5–44
Simulated use of the small space lot on the east side of the model framework. Note: A more private part of the garden is covered with a trellis—a permissible "temporary" structure. Compare this garden and the dwelling with another application of the same site in Figure 4-5. (Steve Zielinsky, University of Oregon, 1975.)

cesses and cycles brings man a sense of affinity with the universal rhythm of life.

The presence of private gardens at upper levels of the framework does not negate the need to go down below. We cannot, however, steal a moment from our other chores to water the tomatoes, if the vegetable plot is three floors below. Unless we live in the lowest level space lots, the grounds take on other meaning. We throw a frisbee there, walk the dog, pick acorns, jog, ride a bike or play tennis, picnic with

neighbors, fly a kite, do more extensive gardening or just wander. Going down, whether to a natural or urban site, becomes an event. No matter how rich the interior environment, there is an occasional need to escape it.

The private garden areas are made possible by the fifteen-foot space truss that supports the "landscape modules" for small trees. There is a differentiation in height of the slab between areas designated as buildable and the rest of the garden. The user could con-

ceivably cover the entire garden area with soil and grow grass, vegetables, and small plants anywhere. The location of the trees, however, has to be predetermined because of the considerable weight and room needed for roots. The place for a tree could be turned into a small swimming pool. The railings too can become continuous or discontinuous planters. Once again, predetermining optimum size of the garden area is not possible, due to varying needs and tastes of future users. As with much of the land of single-family plots, some garden space may be wasted but no garden space need to be maintained only as a right-of-way.

The inner pedestrian street is the lifeline to the space lots (Figures 4–32, 5–43, and 5–47). It not only permits moving of materials, trees, soil, garbage collection, grand pianos, large boats, or sculptures, but it may facilitate the return of street vendors with little battery powered ice cream trucks or music boxes. Conceivably, a framework could even be designed to accommodate personal vehicles, at least the smaller ones, on the inner streets, but the pedestrian nature of the street would then become compromised. In the model framework, cars, motorcycles, and campers will have to be parked in lots or underground garages, but bicycles will be able to roam freely. In sloping terrains, some of the streets could provide a direct connection to the landscape, thereby eliminating the need to use the service elevators for those levels.

The streets are fifteen feet wide, but narrow to ten feet at stair locations (Figures 5–6 and 5–7). The out-of-traffic pockets thus created could contain street furniture, plant life, and so forth to make pleasant places for occasional gatherings. Unless a very high load needs to be moved, there is ample clearance on the street without fear of running into the sloping members.

No street is directly above the other, nor do they go on forever (Figures 5–23 and 5–24). The terracing effect of the streets and the recurring switch to the

Figure 5–45
A detail view of the small space lot on the east side of the model framework (shown in Figure 5–44).

opposite side, which results in change in direction of the street, is inherent in the exploded cuboctahedral order (Figures 5-20 and 5-21). No streets penetrate the cuboctahedra that are zoned for space lots. The streets occupy the A-frame-type space in the tetrahedral–octahedral structure. The V-type of space paralleling the street could over a period of time accommodate additional decks, plants, and other facilities to support the street further.

Perceptually, the streets are not endless but incremental—the living rooms of six space lots (Figures 5-7 and 5-43). The largest available space lots, the complete cuboctahedra, have access to two streets. The terracing of the pedestrian streets facilitates contact between these otherwise horizontal stratifications. People are able to recognize friends a level or two above or below, and occasional glimpses of other areas within the structure give clues of continuity of the framework (Figures 5-46 and 5-47). The streets are 21'-4" apart so that conversation is possible, and the abundance of stairs puts people in easy reach of each other. Since looking directly down on more than two streets at a time is not possible, the fear of heights that some people have should not be a problem. Perhaps only in a few places—from public areas like the special little "parks" and at the vertical circulation cores—should one be able to savor great heights.

Experientially the public places within the framework have the potential to be quite exciting. Space trusses present unparalleled opportunities for spatial experiences. They can absorb a multitude of mechanical systems, special areas, fixtures, plants, flags, suspended membranes, canopies and other surfaces, small enclosed volumes, signs, fountains and all the other things commonly or occasionally found in public places. The contents of no two space lots are likely to be quite the same. The articulation of the

Figure 5-46
Section of the unoccupied model framework (looking north).

facades facing the streets, the amount of enclosure, the personal whims of the residents will contribute to a truly complex and mind-expanding environment.

The pedestrian streets must be animated. They must be supportive of festivals, carnivals, processions, guerrilla theaters, games, block parties, and promenades. To be sure, these activities will not happen everywhere or at all times, but the opportunities for their occurrence must be built in. The idea that the street must be an extension of the users' gardens and living rooms does not imply a return to the medieval lifestyle. Many street activities are timeless, and though they vary from culture to culture and from place to place, the automobile has squeezed them off our American streets. A precedent for such places, however, is the European, Near East, or Oriental street so eloquently described by Bernard Rudowsky.[13]

Unlike the dark, sealed corridor (a perfect place for getting mugged), the open street of the framework is likely to contain a much greater range of daily activity and someone is bound to have it in eyesight most of the time. People will go to and from work and shopping—some on bicycles and some with pushcarts. Children may be playing hopscotch or other games invented for the framework, and a considerable number of maintenance and service personnel will be roaming the structure. The streets will provide easy access to utilities (no need to tear them up here), some of which could run below the streets with other feeder and waste lines that run vertically next to the space lots.

The pedestrian streets are connected with fre-

Figure 5-47
A view of the internal pedestrian street in the model framework. Note: The terracing of the internal pedestrian streets facilitates contact between them. The streets are 21' 4" apart, which makes talking to friends a level above or below possible, and the frequent stairs will put people in easy reach of each other.

quently placed stairs that are also open (Figure 5-6). The stairs are not designed for people to walk up to their homes unless, of course, they live rather close to the ground. While physical fitness enthusiasts may wish to use them all the way up and certainly down, the stairs are placed to facilitate contact between the floors and to minimize the horizontal stratification so characteristic of high-density living. Climbing to a street or two above or below is possible, except for the old and infirm, without going to the circulation core. The stairs in the model framework consist of five flights with landings and bridges between. They are minimal at this time, thereby suggesting the most basic stair. When further developed, they can and will have more extensive landings and connections to detached decks (Figure 5-7).

Stairs are the focal points of public places. The stairway provides an overview of the pedestrian street, a platform for an audience, a place to sit down, a very special view, or a glimpse of a secluded spot. The stairs are not just connectors between two levels but the stage for many other human pursuits.

On a flat site, access to the higher floors of the framework will be through the vertical or perhaps diagonal circulation cores. These cores have not yet been designed, but some of these possibilities were explored in the class projects (Figures 5-15, 5-26, 5-48, and 5-49). Such cores should be located further apart—say, on the order of six hundred feet— than the current practice in high-rise buildings and visualized as extensions of rapid transit systems. A walk less than a block in distance to the closest core is hardly an inconvenience if the core takes on the significance of a three-dimensional intersection. The core is an activity node—a place for social interaction. It should contain an area where people can linger with neighbors or enjoy a very special view rather than merely wait for the elevators in a small and dark lobby.

The very function of the framework rules out such

air-tight widenings in the corridor. Occasionally the cores will have to contain a freight elevator with sufficient space in front of them for maneuvering large loads or the ice cream man's vehicle. The core will also contain two or more passenger elevators, perhaps glass-enclosed, some sort of cart storage area where required, toilets, and a communal space. In all likelihood, ramps between streets could also be incorporated in some instances. The core is an arrival area, and functions appropriate to such areas should be

encouraged.

Concentration of the vertical mode of transportation is also an energy-saving measure. Dispersal of cores results not only in duplication and less efficient use of equipment but also in longer waiting time. In view of our impending energy shortage, use of extensive elevator cores to serve only one high-rise building will have to be reexamined.

The nature of the core at the ground level will vary considerably (Figures 5-16 and 5-49). It will be

Figure 5-48
A large service elevator and a diagonal glass passenger elevator in an offset between two model framework increments. (Jack Hartzell, University of Oregon, 1974.)

determined equally by the core itself, as well as by the particular context. This connection may extend over several levels depending on the makeup of the core and its location. Servicing of the framework will most likely have to be done from a separate level in order to minimize interference with pedestrian activities. Major access to parking, rapid transit, if any, and the landscape in general may be from another level or two.

In order to minimize the detrimental nature of

roads within the site, access and service entrances can be incorporated in the lower levels of the framework. Roads can run between the piers or, in steep sites, on one side of the framework. However, accommodating large parking areas between the supports of such structures is difficult. Pending an environmental or energy disaster, the need for some kind of personal vehicle is likely to persist. The convenience and versatility that this mode of transportation provides is difficult to entirely do away with. The storage

of such vehicles, be they cars or eventually something else, will indeed be with us for some time to come, and the location of parking will have to be looked into during the design of a particular community.

A few words must be said about the ongoing construction and the "incompleteness" of the whole framework. Buildings are often most exciting before they are finished and closed in. Semi-open structures present us with richness in scale and experience seldom matched by the finished construction. Children and adults alike are fascinated. by the construction process, the presence of cranes, and the movement of materials. The framework is a high-density environment where some of that construction would go on from time to time, and the whole milieu would be somewhat reminiscent of a yet-to-be-completed structure. The cranes, of course, would not be there due to the modest scale of building, and disruptions should be minimal.

"Incomplete" use of the space lots will contribute amenities beyond those designed into the framework. Sun may reach some of the gardens and enclosed volumes for a longer period of time if everyone's volume is not closed in to maximum permissible limit. At times, sun could even penetrate the framework from the other side (Figure 4–26). There will be unexpected views through the unfilled part of the space lots of landscape, other frameworks, or more distant neighbors.

The openness to the elements will, no doubt, present the inhabitants with a measure of problems, some unforeseeable. Wind is the most difficult to deal with. The possibility exists that in places the framework could become a wind tunnel. Although models could be tested in wind tunnels and experiments should be conducted with various kinds of openings in the framework, the very premise of this approach to high-density living limits the reliability of such tests. As the occupants can fill in their volumes as much or as little as they please, there is no way to

Figure 5-49
Service access, pedestrian dropoff, and a sloping glass-enclosed passenger elevator below the framework of a student project. (Jack Hartzell, University of Oregon, 1974.)

completely anticipate the conditions of the wind. Even on the same site, the microclimates are likely to vary considerably.

The best way to deal with the problems of the wind and other environmental forces is to tune the framework similar to current acoustical practice. Walls, baffles, temporary or permanent enclosures over some areas, trees, or other elements could counter undesirable wind effects. The whole environment could change with the seasons, and some of it, even daily or instantaneously. On a smaller scale such changes are quite common. In the Japanese house, panels are removed during the humid months to create drafts, and curved bamboo screens are placed against clay walls to protect them from splashing rain. Changes in climate do not pass unnoticed; the presence of natural forces is acknowledged.

The thought of a completely enclosed environment is frightening. Domed cities would deprive man of contact with nature in the name of efficiency. The feel of raindrops, a breeze, or snowflakes and the presence of bees and leaves contribute to the content of our existence as much as other people, events, and work. Few of us relish the thought of battling our way through a storm, but total isolation removes a dimension from our lives.

Although the model framework was designed for moderate climates, open-to-air townframes should be considered for all but the most severe arctic conditions. After all, if the public spaces in the framework are extensions of landscape or townscape and the region is inhabited, the environmental conditions should not be any worse than those presently tolerated in the surrounding urban, suburban, or rural environment. No doubt, some parts of the interior will need to be enclosed and protected, but the life, social interaction, and experience within is contingent on the whole interior being open and continuous.

The openness also eliminates some of the fire hazards and makes application of current fire codes to this framework questionable. If the interior space were closed in, only two floors at a time could be connected because of smoke hazards. Leaving the interior open would permit the smoke and poisonous gases to escape. The multitude of exits, alternate escape routes, and the frequency of stairs would allow for easy exit in the event of a fire. There is no longer any need for closed-in fire stairs, as people could take the stairs away from the source of fire. The current practice of providing enclosed, fire stair towers is not satisfactory. In some buildings, hours would be required to clear the people out due to the inadequacy of the stairs. The smoke would also enter the stairs along with the people trying to get into the stairwell.[14]

Interior volumes on the order of the streets in the framework would require ventilation and air conditioning, thereby making them prohibitively expensive to build and operate. The savings in energy consumption would be considerable in open-to-air frameworks. Infra-red radiant heaters could be installed in some special places where people are likely to gather. Some surfaces may also have to incorporate heating coils for snow and ice elimination. The design of the drainage system for the framework should permit articulation of what otherwise is assigned to subterranian tunnels. Some of the runoff may be used to irrigate the gardens and to supply ponds.

The awareness of the presence of all the mechanical, electrical, and other environmental control systems can be as discreet or open as the inhabitants would prefer. The educational aspect of knowing where everything goes in exposed utility structures is offset by the inevitable ugliness that results in design, subsequent changes and routine maintenance of some services. Certainly, the structure permits integration and easy maintenance of mechanical systems. Change over a period of time is possible in view of the short-term life cycle of mechanical and electrical systems. There are no central air-handling facilities because a framework of this kind would increase the size of ducts and thus render this approach uneconomical. An individual mechanical room on each space lot could provide space for a water heater and heating and cooling equipment, depending on the system preferred by the owner, which is no different in concept from the arrangement in individual houses. Connections from each space lot can be made to the municipal or communal utilities for gas, water, sewer, power, telephone, cable TV, and any other conceivable future service. Energy could be produced by solar radiation or wind, and sewage could be recycled more easily on a communal scale, but how each user handles his own immediate environment would be left to the users of the framework.

The psychological aspects of living off the ground within the framework will have to be examined in greater detail. Hitherto, such studies have focused on high-rise towers and the social isolation that results from living in these structures. However, since we can only examine what is in existence and since the majority of available models, regardless of their height, are psychologically detrimental, the "what if" attitude has governed the design of the model framework. It would have to be built, lived in over a period of time, and evaluated. At this time we can certainly react against the known negative aspects of high-rise living, but the pressures to build high are too real in many parts of the world to ignore them.

Being off the ground or living on mountain slopes has been associated with status. Steep slopes have been inhabited either by the poor or the very rich. The more supportive high-density environments such as Safdie's Habitat in Montreal, penthouses, and other terraced apartments are always in great demand. People living off the ground are compensated with views and fresh breezes. The commotion and noise below can be left behind. The complexities of modern life force people to escape to the countryside, but this luxury is seldom attainable for the majority of the population. Packed together in high-rise towers, people tend to withdraw; subjected to crowds, we long for solitude. The framework should permit withdrawal and contemplation, as well as the more often recognized need for social contact.

IMPLEMENTATION

The question that must be faced is: What will bring the model and similar frameworks about? Building the model framework is possible today. Although it may look futuristic to those not knowledgeable about such structures, there are no excessive technical problems. Despite the fact that no such structures exist, building user-completed frameworks is not only technically possible, it is necessary. Earlier arguments should attest to that. Furthermore, progressing beyond theoretical studies is impossible unless they are put to a test.

User-completed housing frameworks can be undertaken by a private developer or the government. As stated in Chapter 2, public authorities have sufficient power to cut through bureaucracies. On the other hand, private investment could capitalize on the advertising potential of such frameworks and proceed with greater efficiency and determination. The "new-concept-in-living" approach should be most attractive to developers regardless of the scale of the framework. A definite location, market and population studies, financing arrangements, timing of the phases of construction, and so forth would in turn determine the nature of the framework as much as the internal requirements. In the past, new directions have been set by the elite models that were widely copied and adapted. The framework concept is equally applicable to pilot public housing projects as it is to private development. Some of these possibilities, albeit crudely, were suggested by the Operation Breakthrough proposals (Figure 5-50).

At this time there is no effective mechanism for communal decision making on the scale necessary to build such neighborhoods. In the absence of built examples, people are likely to be quite timid about venturing into the unknown. Involving the wider community in the initial plan may be difficult without users who have experienced life in a townframe community. Thus, built examples of the framework are necessary prerequisites to any meaningful community involvement.

Communities have not been given viable alternatives to high-rises, PUD's, and so forth. This author is confident that if presented with a set of possible solutions to projected housing needs and educated in the available choices, people will choose proposals that permit them to control their immediate environment. As the framework grows, the users can play an increasing role in future additions, planning of supporting facilities, and establishment of standards for space-lot use.

The degree of choice in the nature of the infil and the use of the space lots is, of course, dependent on the tolerance of the society and the values of the inhabitants. Any organized society or municipality, be it a commune, a tribal village, a condominium or a neighborhood, adopts use and maintenance standards intended to protect the health and welfare of the individual members of that community. Such standards always protect some and infringe on the choice of others no matter how well intentioned. Within the framework, some safeguards, such as location of privacy barriers or fire walls, should be built in; others will have to be agreed upon and enforced by the inhabitants, or they may evolve through the use of the framework. These, for example, would include the amount of combustible infil material, size of trees, cleaning and repairing of public places, maintenance of grounds, and recycling of materials and waste. The confined root structure may well limit tree size. If the trees, however, manage to grow too big, they may exceed the permissible weight limit on the structure or increase the wind load. Some safety crew or perhaps a computer may have to suggest pruning or replacement of such trees. The inhabitants could conceivably organize an advisory board to help those who do not know what and how to plant and build. With the increase in neighborhood asssociations, a spirit of cooperation tends to replace once adversary relationships between neighbors.

Financing of user-adapted frameworks could be compared to construction of artificial land. The cost of the structure, access systems, and all given utilities and surfaces is similar to the cost of land, the improvements on that land, and the expense of extending municipal service boundaries. This comparison, however, is not entirely just. It does not take into account the elimination of agricultural land, wildlife, and other natural resources. The destruction of countryside through two-dimensional sprawl is difficult to assess financially. The trouble and expense of building frameworks of this height is justified if the surrounding urban context has similar densities or if such concentration will preserve a good part of the environment.

If the framework is to last for say two hundred years or much longer, it may still have to be amortized over a thirty-year period. Depreciating the investment in a seven- or fifteen-year period should not, however, be possible. The tax policy is responsible for much of the ticky-tacky apartment buildings, houses, and roadside developments.

Regardless of the financing, such user-adapted frameworks are going to be less expensive in the long run. Building for permanence and insistence on quality in at least a part of the built environment should be public policy. After all, some residential environments in the United States, such as Beacon Hill in Boston, and countless places in Europe and elsewhere have remained in use for centuries. Perpetual rebuilding has not been required to prudently used resources.

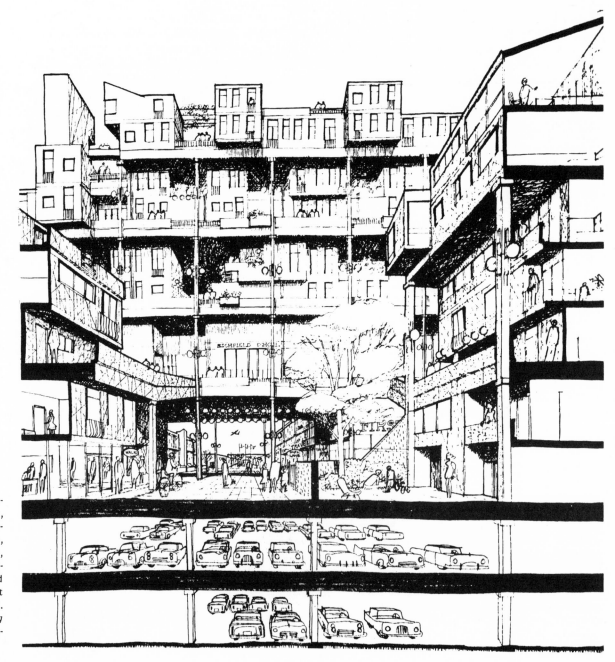

Figure 5-50
"Townland" proposal for Operation Breakthrough by Townland Marketing and Development Corporation with Warner, Burns, Toan, and Lunde, Architects. Note: A precast concrete structure for placement of three-story individual homes, apartments, or townhouses with public streets and planting, the proposal was intended for urban renewal of new developments up to 150 feet high. Although it was not conceived as a user-completed framework, it does nevertheless point the way toward the feasibility of townframes. (See U.S. Department of Housing and Urban Development, *Housing Systems Proposals for Operation Breakthrough* [Washington, D.C.: U.S. Government Printing Office, 1970].)

The construction industry would also be affected by the phasing of construction and separation of long- and short-term building. For one, construction of the frameworks could be shared by large-scale companies and conglomerates and small independent businesses. The task of producing and erecting the space truss structure and the major access roads and pedestrian streets with the other given surfaces would likely fall to large well-established companies with the necessary experience.

The individual space-lot infil, however, would give a chance to the smaller companies and family-run businesses. The subsequent additions and changes in particular would not interest major construction concerns. Much, of course, is dependent on the nature of the infil system. If the framework uses some kind of high-technology system exclusively, the role of construction concerns is limited to erection and assembly; yet it may further much competition in design and manufacture of such kits. A whole new branch of the building industry—user manipulable environmental system—would come into existence and could cater to worldwide markets. In place of cars and bombers, housing systems could become the major export items of some of the highly industrialized countries. At the other end of the scale, the use of current handicraft building methods results in much work within the framework. This approach can be used anywhere today. Some owners may even do their own building, and the small enterprises often confined to construction in suburban and rural areas could compete for these jobs.

The optimum condition, as stated in Chapter 1, would be a highly coordinated building industry that

would not only provide an infinite variety of inter-changeable components but also accept personal modifications and handicraft techniques. The user could not only return unneeded components to some second-hand spare part lot but also exchange one manufacturer's wall system for some other—as we change appliances today—or substitute it with a wall of his own design and making. This pattern is now happening with our cars and miscellaneous trucks; yet the vehicles are much more restrictive, and personal modifications have to conform to rigid safety requirements (Figures 5–51 and 5–52).

Participation in the design and construction of one's house would bring man into a more intimate emotional relationship with his shelter. The increasing amount of leisure time and interest in crafts and even sophisticated technological systems could be focused on organizing, assembling, and constructing the dwellings within the space lots. The love and care currently centered on the nomadic vehicles, building and furnishing of geodesic domes, and alternate energy sources give some assurance that similar endeavors could take place within the context of the framework.

To an ever increasing segment of the population, self-help methods are the only means to shelter. According to William Grindley, 20 percent of single-family dwellings and 12 percent of housing units

Figure 5–51
A user-adapted bus. Note: The love and care devoted to rebuilding of trucks and buses in nomadic homes attest to design skills and pride in craftsmanship. Boats receive similar attention, and many a house harbors hidden modifications.

started in the United States in 1972 were owner controlled.[15] All indications suggest that the percentage is much higher today due to escalating housing costs. In much of the developing world extreme self-help techniques including extra-legal squatting are the only means to housing for all except the very rich.

The nature of the infil and the amount of participation by the inhabitants depend on the social structure of the community. These aspects, no doubt, will be subjected to values and prejudices hardly different from those that currently result in similar population dynamics. Some parts of the framework are likely to become communes, while others become middle-class strongholds or more fashionable neighborhoods. Differences in values will, in turn, affect the nature of future frameworks. The ghetto is the product of economic and social conditions, not architecture.

CONCLUSION

As an extension of the natural environment the framework is, no doubt, artificial, but then so are our subdivisions, not to mention urban housing. Often not even an inch of soil remains of the original environment. Every time man builds, he creates artificial sites, but this artificiality has been so extensive and destructive that little remains of natural patterns. The very environment as we know it is threatened. Le Corbusier recognized this:

Figure 5-52
The rear end of a user-adapted bus. Note: Custom-made vehicles and modified trucks and buses have to conform to safety requirements dictated by the width of the road, yet creativity is much less encumbered by complex and restrictive building codes and ordinances. The more manageable handicraft techniques are often preferred to materials and methods compatible with the initial product. Contrasts albeit extreme are not necessarily displeasing.

Many savages have immediately created artificial sites (a floor raised above the ground) to avoid floods or scorpions, etc. . . . Ladies and gentlemen, organized society has been making artificial sites from the beginning![16]

Nature is not only the school for interdependence of all patterns but, moreover, the model to the structure of the built environment. An organism that is able to change will survive through adaptation over a long period of time. The structure of nature is hierarchic and holistic. Systems and subsystems are able to change independent of or accompanied by transformations of the larger systems. Building will have to develop similar potential for self-regulation in order to survive. Unfortunately, resource exhaustion rather than decisive action will force us into it. Extreme poverty, not wealth, was instrumental in the development of Japanese architecture, building systems, and aesthetic sensibilities.

The aesthetic nature of the permanently incomplete—the imperfect—communicates the process. It involves the user and the observer who completes and refines the environment in his or her mind, as well as through decision making or actual building. Participation, whether perceptually, experientially, or actually physically is absolutely essential if man is to feel at home in his environment. He can not remain a visitor, an uninvolved bystander, or a passive cog in the system. He must feel that he contributes to building his world. The perfect environment or the state of mind is an elusive goal. It cannot be retained for any length of time, but the process to it constitutes life.

Figure 5-53
The unoccupied model framework (looking southwest). Note: Piranesian environs and crisp geometries become hanging gardens. One can identify with the legendary past cultures and myths or the emerging landscapes of the micro world.

The environment must retain some sense of mystery. The framework lends itself to a range of expressions from the bold or overpowering to the matter of fact and subdued (Figures 5-53 and 5-54). The design and construction within each space lot will in turn range from the ordinary and predictable to the refined or ambiguous. The rational must be tempered by the undefinable and unexpected. User-completed townframes are time and space frames through which human existence can manifest itself.

Figure 5-54
The unoccupied model framework (looking northwest). Note: There are few cultural associations and precedents to the west side of the model framework. Past technologies did not permit us to build such cliff-like structures. Is it a contemporary Mesa Verde with additional dwellings carved out of the rock or a crystalline froth spreading like a growth?

Postscript

As may be obvious to the thoughtful reader, there is much more to the idea of townframes, frameworks, and space lots than what has been presented and tested through the simulated applications. The more we explore this area, the more questions arise. Considerable amount of work remains to be done. There is no doubt about this fact.

One hesitates to release a study that is incomplete in its theoretical basis and, particularly, in its suggested and built examples. The danger of misinterpretation is ever present. Yet by making it public, others may contribute to it through criticism, extension, or parallel studies. The task may thus be less lonely.

Hopefully, the work reported in this volume will accelerate building of space-lot frameworks, or the fragments of townframes. Consequently, emphasis has been placed on prevailing modes of living that are not dependent on radical social changes. The framework described in Chapter 5 relies on systems and technologies in existence or buildable today. The image of the future is founded on today's reality—a reality long overdue.

There is a groundswell in "radical" alternative technologies. Much emphasis has been placed on owner-built homes and small, autonomous methods in energy generation. These are most interesting developments, yet despite their contributions, many alternative dwellings are symptoms of escapism. Their very existence usually depends on industrial technology. In the West such alternatives are products of affluence possible only in technologically advanced countries; the builders are living on the fringe of this society and off its waste. Rejection of "the system" *en masse* would not only result in termination of prevailing values and life styles, but survival would require drastic transformations of the alternative beyond current models. Individual little shelters would, for example, further use up valuable land with all the innumerable consequences.

It is not possible to build a solar collector from junk in Guatemala because there is no junk. Self-help projects are well tested and effective in third world countries. In many places this is the only means to a shelter. In these parts of the world self-help projects can not be considered as alternatives but as dominant housing methods. They are the realistic and advanced technologies for these economies.

Today it is fashionable to criticize the modern movement in architecture, and this book too has picked on some of its objects. The modern movement, however, is inseparable from the social and political movements at the time. Architects had also begun to develop social consciousness; the practice of architecture was no longer the exclusive privilege of the rich and the ruling class. The movement gained impetus as a reaction against the sham monuments of the establishment. Architects strived to make their services available to the masses, and they saw industrialization as the means to distribute these services.

The modern movement was suppressed by threatened dictatorships or corrupted by the corporate state. Once again eclecticism is creeping into architecture. Anything goes, and the schools of architecture lack will and vision to rise to the occasion. These are sweeping generalizations, but architecture lacks an overriding direction that would absorb and integrate the various developments that are each in their own way quite interesting.

We need to take stock of the course of architecture. A revolution in architecture is impossible without corresponding social movements, and a revolution can not be prescribed. Revolutions are explosions brought about by a series of cumulative events, but there is no clearly discernible focus to our efforts at this time. At most, architects may get caught up in social, economic, and political upheavals. They are unlikely instigators and advocates of social change.

At their best, architects have not only given material expression to an age but articulated worthy goals and provided models to society.

Notes

CHAPTER 1
AN ARGUMENT

1. Perhaps the best definition of a system is A. D. Hall's statement: "A system is a set of objects with relationships between the objects and between their attributes." See Arthur D. Hall, *A Methodology for Systems Engineering* (Princeton, N.J.: Van Nostrand, 1962), p. 60.
2. Christopher Alexander, *Notes on the Synthesis of Form* (Cambridge, Mass.: Harvard University Press, 1964), p. 41.
3. See Heinrich Engel, *The Japanese House* (Rutland, Vt.: Tuttle, 1964), for the most exhaustive study of the Japanese house and its significance.
4. N. J. Habraken, *Supports*, trans. by B. Valkenburg (New York: Praeger, 1972), p. 14.
5. Ibid., p. 12.
6. Robert Goodman, *After the Planners* (New York: Simon and Schuster, 1971), p. 173. © 1971 by Robert Goodman. Reprinted by permission of Simon & Schuster, Inc.
7. It was brought to my attention that the term *townframe* was used for a project of that title by Michael Buckley and Michael Guran and published by the Department of Architecture, Massachusetts Institute of Technology in *ReseARCH* III, no. 1 (December 1971). The coincidence reassures the likelihood that the term *townframe* can become a generic label of such frameworks. I would, however, like to acknowledge the relatedness of some of the thoughts that went into this work to Michael Guran's experiments. We had a number of discussions, and he explored some of these issues while our teaching at the University of Oregon (1969–70) coincided. See Michael Guran, "Designing for Change: Some Experiments," *Industrialization Forum* 1, no. 2 (January 1970): 33–40.
8. The term *space lots* has been borrowed from Eckhard Schulze-Fielitz, *Urban Systems*, vols. I and II (Stuttgart: Karl Kraemer, 1971 and 1973, respectively).
9. Habraken, *Supports*.
10. Goodman, *After the Planners*, p. 115.
11. Ibid., p. 208.

CHAPTER 2
TOWNFRAMES VERSUS MEGASTRUCTURES

1. "We call them omnibuildings rather than megastructures, because it is not their *mega* quality (great, mighty) which is important, but rather their *omni* (all) aspect that is of interest." See Jan C. Rowan, "Editorial," *Progressive Architecture* XLIX, no. 7 (July 1968): 91.
2. See Reyner Banham, *Megastructure* (New York: Harper & Row, 1976), for the history and review of the development of "Megastructure International."
3. See Kisho Kurokawa's "Hawaii Dreamland," an entertainment and "leisure-time" center near Yamagata. There are a number of other "dreamlands."
4. "Omnibuildings," *Progressive Architecture* XLIX, no. 7 (July 1968): 94.
5. See Wolfgang Braunfels, *Monasteries of Western Europe*, trans. by Alastair Laing (Princeton, N.J.: Princeton University Press, 1972).
6. Friedman's work has appeared in many periodicals. For "Spatial Town," see *Progressive Architecture* XLV, no. 10 (October 1964): 170–71. The underlying arguments are published in Yona Friedman, *Toward a Scientific Architecture* (Cambridge, Mass.: MIT Press, 1975).
7. Ibid.
8. Manfredi G. Nicoletti, "The End of Utopia," *Perspecta: The Yale Architectural Journal* 13/14 (1971): 269–79.
9. "Louis I. Kahn: Talks With Students," *Architecture at Rice* 26 (1969): 24.
10. For a description of some of these, see Robert Goodman, *After the Planners* (New York: Simon and Schuster, 1971), p. 152.
11. Quoted from Robert Venturi *Complexity and Contradiction in Architecture* (New York: The Museum of Modern Art, 1966), p. 46.
12. The figures are from a flyer prepared by *Habitat*, The United Nations Conference on Human Settlements, Vancouver, 1976.
13. Aldo van Eyck in *Team 10 Primer*, ed. by Alison Smithson (Cambridge, Mass.: MIT Press, 1968), p. 100.
14. James T. Burns, Jr., "Social and Psychological Implications of Megastructures," in *Arts of the Environment*, ed. by Gyorgy Kepes (New York: George Braziller, 1972), p. 138.
15. Otto Piene, *More Sky* (Cambridge, Mass.: MIT Press, 1973), preface.
16. The term *habitability* was coined by NASA and is defined by T. M. Fraser, professor of biomedical engineering, as a state of equilibrium that results from "the interactions among the components of a man-machine-environment-mission complex which permits man to maintain physiological homeostasis, adequate performance and acceptable social relationships." See "Space

in Space," *Progressive Architecture* L, no. 11 (November 1969): 135.

17. Fumihiko Maki, *Investigations in Collective Form*, Special Publication No. 2 (St. Louis: Washington University, 1964). Maki's definitions are: "The megastructure is a large frame in which all the functions of a city or part of a city are housed" (p. 8) and "Group-Form . . . is form which evolves from a system of generative elements in space" (p. 14).

18. Ibid., p. 19.

19. Jan C. Rowan, "Editorial," *Progressive Architecture* XLIX, no. 7 (July 1968): 91. Reprinted from *Progressive Architecture*, copyright July 1968, Reinhold Publishing Company.

20. Ibid.

21. J. B. S. Haldane, "On Being the Right Size," in *The World of Mathematics*, ed. by James R. Newman (New York: Simon and Schuster, 1956), vol. 2, p. 954.

22. "Optimizing the Structure of the Skyscraper," *Architectural Record* 152, no. 4 (October 1972): 97–104.

23. Peter S. Stevens, *Patterns in Nature* (Boston: Little, Brown, and Company in Association with Atlantic Monthly Press, 1974), p. 23.

24. See the chapter entitled "The Skyscraper in the Future," in James M. Fitch, *American Building*, 2nd ed. (Boston: Houghton Mifflin, 1966), vol. 1, pp. 290–98.

CHAPTER 4
SOME CRITERIA FOR HIGH-DENSITY SPACE LOTS

1. Christopher Alexander, Sara Ishikawa, and Murray Silverstein, *A Pattern Language*, a manuscript and a forthcoming (Oxford University Press) book. Many of the patterns, however, are value based and unapplicable or contradictory to the goals of this work. Alexander does not recognize the realities of modern urban life, the social–political–economic conditions and construction patterns that have evolved through millennia of building practice.

2. William Kleinsasser, "Experiential Design Considerations," class notes, University of Oregon, 1975.

3. We are concerned here with major physical and psychological interferences and not with elimination of all possible conflicts. No known method short of complete isolation will, for example, eliminate acoustical problems during construction or some other disturbance that may affront the senses. Awareness of many such processes is not necessarily undesirable and may well be an essential part of one's life.

4. Rigid bending-resistant structure systems are ill suited to such loads and through their added mass alone far exceed the weight of such landscape modules.

5. These gardens are certainly artificial but so, to a large degree, are most manmade landscapes. The difference is that the trees along the streets or in gardens have their roots embedded in the ground rather than in containers. There are many trees that do not attain large size and that are well suited for such gardens. Planting of such trees should be encouraged. If, however, the inhabitants insist on planting other varieties, the trees would have to be pruned and trained as is customary with many species or be replaced when their size exceeds permissible weight and wind load limits or their roots fill the container.

6. The framework has been designed for the Northern Hemisphere and a moderate climate similar to Pacific Northwest. Criteria in other parts of the world, such as the need to provide shade rather than exposure to sun, would necessitate different frameworks.

7. The precise sun patterns can, of course, be plotted with models or computers, which would be of help to the users. However, incomplete construction within the space lots and the surprises from reflections will provide additional and unpredictable views or sunlight and may well render such exercises academic.

CHAPTER 5
THE FRAMEWORK

1. Le Corbusier, *The Radiant City* (New York: The Orion Press, 1967).

2. Alison and Peter Smithson, "Signs of Occupancy," *Architectural Design* 43, no. 2 (February 1972): 91–97.

3. Kiyonori Kikutake, "Challenge to Mass-housing," *The Japan Architect* 47, no. 6 (June 1972): 23–33.

4. "Symbol Zone," *The Japan Architect* 45, no. 5/6 (May–June 1970): 36–48.

5. "Spatial Town," *Progressive Architecture* XLV, no. 10 (October 1964).

6. Eckhard Schulze-Fielitz, *Urban Systems*, vols. I and II (Stuttgart: Karl Kraemer, 1971 and 1973, respectively).

7. Guntis Plesums, "Architecture and Structure as a System," *Architecture Canada* 46, no. 4 (April 1969): 23–33.

8. Robert Venturi, *Complexity and Contradiction in Architecture* (New York: The Museum of Modern Art, 1966).

9. "Precast, Prestressed Concrete Trusses Carry a Hangar Roof," *Engineering News-Record*, August 13, 1959, pp. 32–36.

10. "Tinkertoy Houses," *The Architectural Forum* 130, no. 1 (January–February 1969): 96–99.

11. Moshe Safdie, *For Everyone a Garden* (Cambridge, Mass.: MIT Press, 1974).

12. The term *internal street* was first used by Le Corbusier; see *The Radiant City*.

13. Bernard Rudofsky, *Streets for People* (New York: Doubleday, 1969).

14. Marguerite Willecco, "Highrise Fires Alarm the Building Industry," *The Architectural Forum* 136, no. 2 (March 1972): 52–55.

15. William C. Grindley, "Owner-Builders: Survivors with a Future," in *Freedom to Build*, ed. by John C. Turner and Robert Fichter (New York: Macmillan, 1972).

16. Le Corbusier, *The Radiant City*, p. 56.

Index